Outdoor Gas Griddle Cookbook

3700 days of Easy, Tasty, and Affordable Griddle Everyday Recipes to Take Your Griddling Skills to The Next Level and Astonish Your Friends and Family

Thomas K. Clark

© Copyright 2023 by Thomas K. Clark - All rights reserved.

This document is geared towards providing exact and reliable information regarding the topic and issue covered. The publication is sold with the idea that the publisher is not required to render accounting, officially permitted, or otherwise, qualified services. If advice is necessary, legal or professional, a practiced individual in the profession should be ordered.

- From a Declaration of Principles, which was accepted and approved equally by a Committee of the American Bar Association and a Committee of Publishers and Associations.

In no way is it legal to reproduce, duplicate, or transmit any part of this document in either electronic means or printed format. Recording of this publication is strictly prohibited, and any storage of this document is not allowed unless with written permission from the publisher. All rights reserved.

The information provided herein is stated to be truthful and consistent, in that any liability, in terms of inattention or otherwise, by any usage or abuse of any policies, processes, or directions contained within is the solitary and utter responsibility of the recipient reader. Under no circumstances will any legal responsibility or blame be held against the publisher for any reparation, damages, or monetary loss due to the information herein, either directly or indirectly.

Respective authors own all copyrights not held by the publisher.

The information herein is solely offered for informational purposes and is universal. The presentation of the information is without contract or any guarantee assurance.

The trademarks used are without any consent, and the trademark publication is without permission or backing by the trademark owner. All trademarks and brands within this book are for clarifying purposes only and are owned by the owners, not affiliated with this document.

Contents

Introduction 11

Chapter 1: Introduction to the Outdoor Gas Griddle 12
    1.1 How to Select the Best Outdoor Gas Griddle 13
    1.2 Components of Outdoor Gas Griddle 14
    1.3 Advantages of Using an Outdoor Gas Griddle 15
    1.4 Health Advantages of Using an Outdoor Gas Griddle 17

Chapter 2: How to Use the Outdoor Gas Griddle 18
    2.1 Preparing the Griddle 18
    2.2 Maintenance Tips 20
    2.3 Griddle Accessories 20
    2.4 Pro Suggestions 21

Outdoor Gas Griddle Temperature Chart 23

Conversion Tables of the Various Units of Measurement 24

Chapter 3: Breakfast Recipes 25
    1. Breakfast Sandwich with Bacon and Swiss Cheese 25
    2. French Toast Sticks 26
    3. Porcini Mushrooms, Garlic and Bacon Omelet 27
    4. Sausage and Veggie Scramble 28
    5. Avocado and Egg Breakfast Burrito 29
    6. Ricotta Cheese and Pistachio Sandwich 30
    7. Oatmeal Breakfast Bars 30
    8. Egg White Breakfast Bites 31
    9. Whole meal and Cocoa Pancake 32
    10. Charred Bread with Ricotta and Cherry Salsa 33
    11. Breakfast Burritos with Green Salsa 33
    12. Breakfast English Muffin Strata 34
    13. Mini Breakfast Quiches 35
    14. Fluffy Blueberry Pancakes 37
    15. Italian Egg, Sausage and Cheese Crunch Wrap 38
    16. Veggie Breakfast Cakes 39

17. Breakfast Potato Boats 40

18. Breakfast Enchiladas 41

19. Gorgonzola and Figs Toast 41

20. Hearty Breakfast Muffins 42

Chapter 4: Burger Recipes 44

1. Barbecue Cheese Burgers 44

2. Italian Hamburgers 45

3. Asian Turkey Burgers 45

4. Cuban Frita Burgers 46

5. German Burgers 47

6. Middle Eastern Turkey Kibbeh Burgers 48

7. Spicy Tofu and Pork Burgers 49

8. Open-Faced Lone Star Burgers 50

9. Key West Burgers 50

10. Crunchy Chicken Burgers 51

11. Mexican Burgers 52

12. Grilled Summer Burgers 53

13. Smoked Trout Burgers with Horseradish and Ricotta 53

14. Tex-Mex Burgers 54

15. Bulgarian Burgers 54

16. Seekh Kebab Burgers 55

17. Asian Salmon Burgers 56

18. Bacon-Gouda Burgers 56

19. Chicken Marsala Burgers 58

20. Bean & Chile Burgers 58

Chapter 5: Vegetarian and Side Dish Recipes 60

1. Creamy Grilled Potato Salad 60

2. Easy Fried Rice 61

3. Spinach Salad with Tomato Melts 62

4. Green Beans in Mustard Sauce 62

5. Roasted Broccoli with Parmesan 64

6. Tofu Skewers with Spicy Peanut Sauce 65

7. Zucchini Almond and Gouda Meatballs 66

8. Peas and Cheddar Pie 67
9. Eggplant and Ricotta Bundles 68
10. Romaine Salad with Bacon & Blue Cheese 69
11. Thyme Potato Focaccia 70
12. Tofu and Ginger Stuffed Yellow Bell Peppers 71
13. Soy Cheese and Bell Pepper Gazpacho 72
14. Grilled Potato Chips with Lemon Mustard Sauce 73
15. Ratatouille 75
16. Glazed Tofu Steaks with Mango Salsa 76
17. Balsamic-Glazed Veggie Kabobs 77
18. Gorgonzola and Potatoes Gratin 78
19. Smoked Cheesy Eggplant 79
20. Zucchini and Tomato Quiche 80
21. Stuffed Yellow Bell Peppers 81
22. Garlic, Bacon & Lemon Cauliflower Steaks 82
23. Cauliflower and Spicy Cheddar Soufflé 83
24. Cumin Chili Potato Wedges 85
25. Parmesan-Garlic Asparagus 86

Chapter 6: Appetizers, Snacks, and Desserts 87
1. Southwest Chicken Drumsticks 87
2. Corn Cakes 87
3. Apple Cobbler 88
4. Caramel Bananas 89
5. Smashed Cheddar Bacon Baby Potatoes 89
6. Crispy Kale Chips 91
7. Pumpkin Pie 91
8. Chewy Peanut Butter Cookies 92
9. Bacon Cheddar Slider 92
10. Loaded Tater Tots 93
11. Brownie Bread Pudding 94
12. Chocolate Chip Mint Cookies 96
13. Tortilla Pizza 96
14. Loaded Nachos 97

15. Apple Pear Crisp 98

16. Soft Gingerbread Cookies 99

17. Chili Con Queso 100

18. Stuffing Turkey Bacon Balls 100

19. Caramel Pecan Brownie 101

20. Cherry Cobbler 102

21. Sausage Mini Rolls 103

22. Southwestern-Style Stuffed Peppers 104

23. Caramelized Bourbon Pears 105

24. Irish Coffee Pie 106

25. Asparagus Wrapped in Bacon 108

26. Parmesan-Herb Popcorn 109

27. Lemon Bars 109

28. Blueberry Buckle Coffee Cake 111

29. Atomic Buffalo Turds 112

30. Loaded Potatoes 114

Chapter 7: Fish and Seafood Recipes 116

1. Roasted Sheet Pan Salmon with Spring Vegetables and Pesto 116

2. Spicy Asian BBQ Shrimp 117

3. Lobster Tails with Citrus Butter 118

4. Scallops with Lemony Salsa Verde 119

5. Tuna Meatloaf with Lemon and Capers 120

6. Spiced Snapper with Mango and Red Onion Salad 121

7. Cedar-Plank Salmon with Mango Salsa 122

8. Seafood Ceviche 123

9. Roasted Stuffed Rainbow Trout with Brown Butter 125

10. Roasted Halibut with Tartar Sauce 126

11. Oysters with Tequila Butter Skillet 127

12. Parsley Herbed Fish Stew 128

13. Sweet Mustard Calamari 129

14. Swordfish with Corn Salsa 130

15. Teriyaki Salmon 131

16. Mexican Shrimp 131

17. Citrusy Clams with Tomatoes & Chickpeas 132

18. White Wine Shrimp Scampi 133

19. Garlicky Salmon with Avocado Salsa 134

20. Crab Cakes 135

21. Oysters with Spiced Tequila Butter 135

22. Gremolata Swordfish Skewers 137

23. Halibut Fillets with Spinach and Olives 138

24. Tuna with Pistachio Sauce 139

25. Halibut Fillets with Lemon and Butter Sauce 140

Chapter 8: Poultry Recipes 142

1. Creole Chicken Stuffed with Cheese & Peppers 142

2. Classical Chicken Meatballs in Hot Sauce 143

3. Grilled Chicken with Fruit Salsa 144

4. Wild Duck Breast 145

5. Turkey in Herb Sauce 146

6. Teriyaki Chicken and Veggie Rice Bowls 147

7. Tender & Sweet Chicken Skewers 148

8. Citrusy Goose Breast 149

9. Moroccan Chicken 150

10. Chicken Satay in Almond Butter Sauce 151

11. Goose and Kraut 152

12. BBQ Chili Smoked Turkey Breast 153

13. Maple Bourbon Turkey 154

14. Stuffed Gouda Chicken Meatloaf 155

15. Pears and Pine Nuts Stuffed Chicken 156

16. Duck with Soy, Honey, and Ginger 157

17. Turkey Breast Noodles with Ginger and Parsley 158

18. Cumin Spiced Turkey Breast 159

19. Roasted Duck 161

20. Sweet Mesquite Seasoned Chicken Breasts 162

21. Apple, Rocket, and Pistachio Grilled Chicken 163

22. Lemon Ginger Chicken with Fruit Salsa 164

23. Duck Adobo 165

24. Smoked Marinated Turkey Breast 165
25. Wine and Thyme Turkey Stew 167

Chapter 9: Beef, Pork, and Lamb Recipes 168
1. Beef Steak with Curry Sauce and Pine Nuts 168
2. Roast Beef Stuffed with Spinach and Speck 169
3. Grilled Ranch Pork Chops with Peach Jalapeno Salsa 170
4. Moroccan Spiced Pork Tenderloin with Creamy Harissa Sauce 171
5. Lamb Lollipops with Mango Chutney 172
6. Roasted Lamb with Root Vegetables 174
7. Classic Beef Stew 175
8. Rack of Beef with Potatoes and Mushrooms 176
9. Texas-Style Brisket 178
10. Double-Cut Grilled Pork Chop with Sweet & Sour Peaches 179
11. Pork Skewers with Avocado and Cherry Tomatoes 180
12. Lamb with Mint Orange Sauce 181
13. Lamb Loaf 182
14. Moroccan-Spiced Rack of Lamb 183
15. Beef Chili 185
16. Tuscan-Style Steak with Crispy Potatoes 186
17. Pork Skewers with Apple and Feta 187
18. Pork Chops Stuffed with Cheese 188
19. Habanero-Marinated Pork Chops 189
20. Lamb Chops in Soy Sauce 190
21. Lamb Lollipops with Yuzu Aioli 191
22. Grilled Southwestern Lamb 192
23. Sliced Beef with Asparagus and Honey Sauce 193
24. Beef Meatballs in Sweet and Sour Sauce 194
25. Goulash 195

Chapter 10: Game Meat Recipes 197
1. Smothered Pheasant 197
2. Pheasant Poppers 198
3. Breaded Pheasant Nuggets 198
4. Deer Poppers 199

5. Drunk Deer Chili 200

6. Buffalo Meatloaf 201

7. Colorado Buffalo Chili 202

8. Deer Jerky 203

9. Blue Stuffed Buffalo Burger 204

10. Tender Pheasants 204

11. Venison Fajitas 205

12. Venison Stew 206

13. Venison Mostaccioli Casserole 207

14. Venison Meatloaf 208

15. Sweet and Spicy Cocktail Meatballs 209

16. Sloppy Does 210

17. Bison Stew 211

18. Bison Burgers 212

19. Elk Shepherd's Pie 213

20. Honey-Orange Bison Back Ribs 214

21. Elk Chili 215

22. Roast Pheasant 215

23. Slow Roasted Rabbit 217

24. Chipotle Bison Chili 218

25. Buffalo Veggie Quinoa Meatloaf 219

26. Garlic Rabbit 221

27. Rabbit Loin Cigars 222

28. Rabbit with Sage and Lemon 223

29. Greek Rabbit 224

30. Caribbean Rabbit 224

4-Week Meal Plan 226

Conclusion 230

Recipes Index 231

Introduction

Food preparation for various outdoor activities may be difficult. This is because when you are away from home and outdoors, you may not have access to the necessary culinary equipment and tools. Multiple-burner gas stoves that allow you to cook various foods are a boon. An outdoor gas griddle meets all of these requirements without sacrificing quality. It is made of high-quality stainless steel. Because thick, hot-rolled steel stores and distributes heat energy, you can prepare meals more easily, regardless of your level of expertise. An outdoor gas griddle is a must-have item if you're planning a large outdoor BBQ.

The Griddle is a gas-powered outdoor cooking appliance with a flat top surface that distributes heat steadily and evenly. Everything that can be cooked in a frying pan can be cooked in this machine, including eggs, French toast, home fries, stir-fries, sausages, and bacon. Skilled cooks may also use the Griddle, popular among amateur BBQers. The flat top surface of the object is made of heavy, cold-rolled steel that will not stick, dent, bruise, or corrode. The griddle's legs can be folded, making it easy to transport from one location to another. Griddles, in general, make cooking simple, quick, and efficient.

A griddle is one type of cooking equipment that can be used to prepare food. A "bakestone" or "planc" in Wales, a "girdle" in Scotland, a "plancha" in Spain, a "comal" in Mexico and Central America, and a "teppan" in Japan are all names for what we now call a metal griddle. The griddle is a versatile piece of kitchen equipment that can be used to prepare various dishes. It can cook food that requires stovetop baking for many dishes. The griddle is a cooking equipment used in many countries to cook vegetables, meat, and seafood. Tortillas are cooked on griddle pans in many countries. As griddles make a comeback, griddle cooking recipes are in high demand. Cooking with griddles is simple; the equipment is used to make pancakes, sausages, bacon, eggs, and other dishes. On the griddle, you can even make grilled sandwiches and fajitas. The griddle is a versatile stove that can be used for various recipes. The griddle's history dates back to a time when there were no ovens and people cooked on stovetops. Cooking was traditionally done on flat-top grills made of brick, stone, or clay. People are drawn to the griddle because of its simplicity and ease of use while cooking. People nowadays prefer to cook at home and prefer simple recipes. Using a griddle allows you to cook food in less time and in a more straightforward manner.

Before we get into making delicious recipes with your outdoor gas griddle, it's important to understand what it is, how to use it, some pro tips, and so on. So let's get started!

Chapter 1: Introduction to the Outdoor Gas Griddle

An outdoor gas griddle is a must-have tool for perfectly cooked eggs that don't require flipping. This even-heating device traps the heat from your stovetop and provides seared edges, allowing you to cook for up to four people simultaneously. So, what exactly is an outdoor gas griddle? It's basically the same as cooking with a single large pan or grill; it's great for quick and easy dinners.

Griddles are one of our favorite kitchen items because they can be used to cook almost anything. You can cook pancakes, fry bacon, and even bake a cake in them! They're made of cast iron with a chrome finish, so they keep the heat evenly distributed and are ideal for searing a steak. They are also very simple to store because they fold flat. In reality, it is the best product of its kind.

This kitchen accessory's best feature, in our opinion, is that it is dishwasher-safe! It lacks a rubberized hinge and air vents that would allow heat to escape from the cooking area. This simplifies cleanup and ensures that your food is thoroughly and evenly cooked. It also retains heat for several hours until you require it again.

An outdoor gas griddle is suitable for roasting, searing, frying, and baking. It's also collapsible, making it very easy to store. One of our favorite features is that griddles are made of cast-iron material that has been seasoned with a specific blend of oils to prevent rusting. It's quite durable, making it ideal for use in a frying pan, grill, or on the stovetop.

The standard griddle measures 21 1/2 inches long and has four baking surfaces spaced 12 inches apart. These cast-iron countertop griddles are heat-resistant. They have an easy-to-clean enamel surface that will not rust or stain like traditional cast iron pans. When searing a steak, each surface has a textured finish knob that allows you to control the heat. The griddle is durable and well-made, and it has proven to be resistant to the elements over time. It's also very easy to clean because you can wipe it down with a damp cloth or put it in the dishwasher.

To summarize, a griddle is a fantastic tool for creating a wide range of delectable dishes. It can be used to cook anything from eggs to pancakes to meat without having to move your pan around the cooktop trying to get it to heat up evenly.

1.1 How to Select the Best Outdoor Gas Griddle

The key to enjoying an Outdoor Gas Griddle is to find the right flat top for your needs. This guide will walk you through the various characteristics to consider.

Flat top size

Flat-top griddle sizes typically range from 17 to 22 to 28 to 36 inches.

Consider the number of individuals you will be serving food to and whether you want the griddle to be portable or not when choosing a size.

Gas or Electric

Even though we are primarily discussing gas griddles, you may want to consider an electric griddle. Electric griddles come in a variety of sizes and are suitable for both indoor and outdoor use.

A nonstick simple flat-top griddle surface is featured on electric flat-top griddles. However, gas flat-top griddles must be properly seasoned and cared for. While gas griddles provide a better sear and flavor, electric griddles are much easier to clean afterward. Each griddle series has its own set of benefits and drawbacks, so figure out what works best for you and your family.

Combination Features

Combinations of a gas griddle and a grill are becoming more popular. All of the units include a griddle in various sizes, as well as one of the following features: There are air fryers, deep fryers, side burners, and grills to choose from.

Accessories

There are usually many Accessories to choose from. Softcover, hardcover, cutting board, side shelf, grease management system position, garbage bag holder, with or without stand, locking swivel caster wheels.

1.2 Components of Outdoor Gas Griddle

When you purchase the gas griddle, it comes with a variety of components. Some of the basic components and their applications are as follows.

Griddle Top

One of the main components of the 28-inch flat cooking surface area is the griddle top. It is constructed of thick, cold-rolled steel. The griddle top fits perfectly over the H-shaped gas burners. After thoroughly seasoning your griddle top, you can cook your food on it.

Side Mounted Shelf

The griddle has a side-mounted shelf for holding ingredients, utensils, an oil squeeze bottle, and other items while cooking.

Griddle Legs

The griddle has foldable griddle legs, allowing you to move your griddle wherever you want easily. These legs also have a caster wheel that allows you to adjust the griddle position properly, and the caster wheel has a lock mechanism to keep the griddle stable while cooking your food.

Gas Controller Switch

The gas flame and griddle temperature are managed by a single switch. It has variable speeds, from very high to very low, so that you can tailor it to the specific needs of your recipe. The two gas knobs are completely separate and can be used to cook at two different temperatures simultaneously.

The Ignition Switch

The ignition switch ignites your griddle. It is a battery-powered switch. To automatically fire up the griddle burners, set the gas controller to high and immediately press the ignition switch.

Drip Tray

The removable drip tray is precisely positioned at the bottom side of the griddle and is secured between the griddle's four legs.

1.3 Advantages of Using an Outdoor Gas Griddle

A gas griddle is an excellent way to feed a large group while also keeping your breakfast or lunch establishment busy. With a revolutionary design that incorporates all of the features of a traditional grill, as well as an additional open area for pancakes, eggs, bacon, and more! This flat-top grill has 3 removable stainless steel cooking surfaces. The heated bottom area, with just enough headroom for bread slices and buns, is ideal for cooking classic foods like burgers or sausages.

The center component features 2 fully adjustable burners that can be configured in a "V" configuration or in parallel to accommodate the various pan sizes currently available on the market. The third component is a gas-powered griddle with a cast aluminum top. The gas griddle's heat retention and even cooking temperature ensure consistently excellent cooking results.

This commercial-grade restaurant equipment is ideal for any food service business or a homeowner looking to recreate the restaurant experience at home!

The gas griddle is one of the best options for your outdoor weekend celebrations. It has many benefits, including the following:

Construction of High Quality

A black powder coating layer protects the stainless steel material of the outdoor gas griddle. It protects the griddle from rust, extending its lifespan. The uppermost 28-inch cooking surface plate comprises the thickest 7-gauge cold-rolled steel material. Overall, the materials used to make the outdoor griddle are of high quality.

Cooking with Adaptability

The outdoor gas griddle gives versatile cooking options by simultaneously cooking different items on the flat cooking surface area at different temperatures. It can be used to make tacos, bacon, French toast, pancakes, eggs and cheese sandwiches, and other dishes. For lunch, you can make chicken, burgers, pasta, steak, hotdogs, and other foods. Make outstanding tuna, shrimp, salmon, and other dishes for a stunning meal. With the gas griddle, you can cook like a professional chef for as long as possible.

Surface Area for Cooking: Large and Flat

The gas griddle has a generous 28-inch cooking surface. In a single cooking cycle, it can accommodate 16 steaks, 28 hamburgers, and 72 hotdogs. By gliding the spatula and scraper across the flat griddle cooking surface, you can easily turn your food. One of the primary benefits of having a large cooking surface area is that food does not retain moisture, resulting in crispy results. The gas griddle is one of the best cooking equipment for enjoying weekend parties.

Optimal Temperature Control

The gas griddle comes with a heat control system. It has two separate gas control valves that generate two distinct temperature zones on the flat griddle surface, allowing you to cook food at two different temperatures in the same batch. The gas controller switches have heat settings ranging from high to low.

Cleaning is a Piece of Cake

The greasy portion of the griddle's top cooking surface can be easily cleaned with a scraper or spatula. You can also clean the griddle's top cooking surface with a paper towel. The drip tray collects all of the excess oil and liquids that drip from the food, which you can then empty and wash with soapy water.

Seared and Locked-In Flavor

Searing has been done for centuries. The Aztecs enjoyed searing tortillas over clay flat tops, and the Scots did the same with their scones. It's a cooking technique that produces a wonderful crust on the surface. Take a look at that charred, crispy, and toasty browned steak. That is exactly what sear does, and it is fantastic. Chefs refer to this as the Maillard Reaction. Have you ever dined in a five-star establishment? Steakhouses that serve meat that tastes divinely divine? They most likely used a Griddle because it's the only way to get that precious, delectable crust. Griddles also help to keep the flavors in. How did you conduct your investigation? This is due to the flat surface, which prevents the juices from escaping. They're forced to infuse the flesh, which is ideal! The fat from a griddle is used as a seasoning. That means juicier and more flavorful meats. Put some seasonings on the flat top, and the meat will absorb them immediately - something you won't get with a regular grill.

Portable

Wouldn't it be great if you could cook steakhouse-quality food no matter where you were? What a treat it would be to be able to cook without having to make sacrifices! Griddles, thank goodness! They fold up and are portable, allowing you to cook outside whenever possible! Do you want to cook alongside a mountain? Is that a ship? Would you like to tailgate close to the stadium? What was the name of the park where you played as a kid? A best friend's backyard? Anywhere. Griddles follow you on your journey and have the same effects. All that is required is food, gas, and a griddle. There are also other people to eat with!

Cook in All Seasons

When do people consume barbecue? Isn't it summer already? With a gas griddle, you can make it in any season: summer, winter, fall, and spring. The griddle is up to the task, whether it's a hot summer day or a harsh winter. This is because the griddle runs on propane. A strong wind, on the other hand, will not result in a propane shortage. The burners will not turn off due to the moisture in the air. So, if you want a griddle-cooked winter supper, go for it. So, rain or shine, cold or hot, the griddle cooks any food perfectly.

From Amateur to Professional Chef

Griddles have all of the features that a steakhouse chef needs. And we're talking about the very best. The flat-top has everything you need to infuse precious flavor into every dish. Burners must be precisely controlled. Use high heat for a quick sear. Turn up the volume. How about a low flame for slow cooking? You've got it as well. It is simple for any beginner to learn. The flat top is made of cold-rolled steel. Because of the forging process, heat retention is excellent. You'll never again eat an undercooked dinner. Every dish prepared by griddle is delicious. There's something for everyone, from meat to vegetables. There's something for everyone, from expert Bang Bang Shrimp to a simple Philly Cheesesteak. With our recipes, your dinners will always be a hit! As a result, the griddle is the most versatile and straightforward outdoor cooking device. It has all of the features of a pro but the ease of use of an amateur and the price of a champion. You can't go wrong with griddle!

When should it not be used?

Everyone enjoys food cooked outside, but if you don't have enough outdoor space, you might not be able to use the Griddle. A good rule of thumb is to use the griddle instead of a traditional gas or charcoal grill.

1.4 Health Advantages of Using an Outdoor Gas Griddle

Cooking on the outdoor gas griddle is healthier than cooking on the stovetop or in the oven. We'll go over some of the health advantages. Let's take a look at the top five health benefits.

You are Eating Less Fat

You consume less fat when barbecuing because some of it drips through the grates. Think about how different a burger turns out when cooked on a griddle as opposed to a stovetop. On the stove top or griddle, the fat will melt away. As a result of the lack of drainage, fat from the stovetop pools and is soaked up by the meat.

Griddled Vegetables Are Significantly Better for Your Health

In spite of popular belief, vegetables lose less of their nutritional value when grilled. Vegetables with a low water content fall into this category.

Vegetables tossed on your griddle are usually in season and fresh, making them a better option than canned vegetables. Wrapped in foil or placed directly on top of your griddle, this method of cooking vegetables retains far more of their nutrients than either boiling or frying.

Meat is Nutrient-Dense

More thiamine and riboflavin are actually preserved when cooking a piece of beef on a gas griddle. Both minerals are necessary for a healthy diet and have numerous health benefits.

You're Making Use of Less Butter

If you master the griddle and don't overcook the food, you'll have juicy cuts of the meat and delectable vegetables. As the griddle locks in so much more moisture, you'll find yourself using less butter and other toppings. You cut down on both calorie and unhealthy substance intake.

Outdoor Activities Go Well with Griddling

Griddling is a fun way to spend time outside. Many parents toss a Frisbee or kick the ball across their yard with their children while grilling dinner. Cooking and dining outside encourages more movement, which we all know is a great health benefit to go along with the tasty meal.

Chapter 2: How to Use the Outdoor Gas Griddle

2.1 Preparing the Griddle

After removing the Gas Griddle from its packaging, double-check that you have all of the included parts and fasteners by consulting the user manual.

The operation technique and working mechanism of the advanced gas griddle are identical to those of other classic griddles. The only difference between a traditional and an advanced griddle is that the cooking surface of a traditional griddle must be removed due to direct heat, whereas the cooking top of an advanced griddle does not need to be removed. The griddle has a separate temperature control valve that maintains the desired temperature while grilling your favorite foods. The following step-by-step instructions will show you how to use your griddle with ease.

Before turning on your griddle, ensure the battery is properly inserted into the ignition switch.

Ascertain that the propane gas cylinder is securely connected to the gas pipe. Turn on the gas and release it through the gas control valve.

Turn on your griddle by turning the gas control valve to High and pressing the ignition switch until you see a flame.

For best results, always warm the griddle for 3 to 5 minutes before placing your meal on the frying surface.

You can now cook anything on your griddle.

Suggestions for Pre-Startup

- Check that the griddle plate is properly positioned in the four holes (2 on each side)
- Wipe the cast iron griddle clean and debris-free with a damp cloth, then completely dry it.
- Check that all gas connections are tight and that there are no leaks before you begin cooking.
- Insert the battery into the igniter button. Remove the screw, replace the battery, and tighten it with your fingers.
- Check that all of the shelves (bottom and sides) are securely fastened.
- Check that the casters are in place and that the locks are functional.
- Check that your propane tank is new and has an OPD valve.
- If at all possible, place the griddle in a wind-protected location.

Suggestions for the First Startup

- Check that the griddle plate is properly positioned in the four holes (2 on each side)
- Check that your propane tank is new and has an OPD valve.
- Keep your propane tank at least half full or half empty.
- If at all possible, place the griddle in a wind-protected location.
- Start the propane stove.
- Turn on the left burner to high (near the igniter button).
- Instead of looking down into the space between the griddle and the burners, press the igniter button and listen for the ticking.
- Ticking should be heard, followed by the first burner lighting up. Allow the burner to heat up for 30 seconds.
- Restart the second burner's operation.
- Rep with ALL of the burners till the griddle is fully lit.

2.2 Maintenance Tips

Proper storage and maintenance are required to extend the life of your griddle. The steps below will walk you through storing and maintaining your griddle.

Clean your Griddle After Each Use

When you first start using your griddle, it automatically seasons after each use. Cleaning is an important step in keeping your griddle clean and sanitary. To clean the griddle surface, use hot water and a paper towel. To clean the cooking surface, do not use soapy water. Clean the cooking area with a scrapper. Clean and dry paper towels can be used to clean the greasy surface.

Get Rid of Rust

If you find any rust spots on the griddle, use 40 or 60 low grit sandpaper or steel wool to remove the rust spots and scrub them thoroughly.

After Cleaning, Coat the Griddle

After cleaning, apply a thin coat of cooking spray to the griddle's cooking surface to prevent rust from accumulating on the griddle's overcooking surface area.

Griddle Storage and Care

After you've completed all of the cleaning steps, store your griddle in a cool, dry place. Always keep your griddle covered and away from humid areas to avoid dust.

2.3 Griddle Accessories

The griddle tools are essential accessories for becoming an expert in outdoor griddle cooking. The essential tools are a spatula, a scraper, and an oil and water squeeze bottle. Some griddle accessories, such as a bacon grill press and basting covers, make the cooking process faster and easier.

1. Basic Griddle Equipment

Scrapper Tool

The scraper tool is made of stainless steel and has a sharp blade-like surface. It also has a non-slip wooden handle for a secure grip. The scraper tool is primarily used for digging and scraping. It's used to clean the top cooking surface for derbies, as well as to lift cakes, pies, pizzas, and tarts.

Spatula

The spatula is a flat and broad tool made of strong stainless steel with an ergonomic handle for a secure grip. It is a multipurpose tool used to flip, lift, and mix foods such as omelets, pancakes, eggs, vegetables, and more. You can choose between large, medium, and small spatulas depending on your cooking needs.

Squeeze Bottles

The squeeze bottles are made of BPA-free plastic and are used to spray or squeeze oils, water, and sausage while cooking on the griddle. The bottles are lightweight and perfect for outdoor cooking.

2. Extra Griddle Accessories

Basting Cloth

The basting tool is made of high-quality stainless steel and has a heat-resistant stainless steel handle. It is the ideal tool for steaming vegetables, melting cheese, evenly roasting food, and keeping food warm. Choose a large blasting cover to accommodate the number of patties and food at once.

Grill Press

The grill press is made of heavy cast iron with a wooden handle grip for easy holding. This tool is used to flatten hamburgers, sandwiches, and bacon, as well as a steak weight. The grill press's primary function is to remove excess oil and juices from your food.

2.4 Pro Suggestions

The gas griddle is easy to use; follow the griddle cooking tips and tricks shown below.

Season the Cooking Surface

The stainless steel cooking surface of your Gas Griddle, like that of most high-quality cooking appliances, must be properly seasoned to ensure the best cooking results. "What exactly is seasoning?" you may wonder. Until nonstick coatings were invented, there was only one way to keep food from sticking to the stove surface. By generating a layer of burnt-on oil, you will not only achieve a beautiful nonstick surface, but you will also protect the cooking surface from scratches and oxidation. Let's get this party going. To begin, clean the cooking surface thoroughly with soap and water. Use a cloth to dry the surface. After that, add a small amount of oil to the frying surface. The best oils to use are vegetable or canola oils with a high smoke point. Using a paper towel, spread the oil evenly across the frying surface. Set the temperature to 275°F and light all four burners. Wait for the oil to start smoking and the surface to darken before proceeding. After the griddle begins to smoke, turn off the burners and allow it to cool. Rep this step two or three more times until the entire area is black. Your griddle is now nonstick and corrosion-resistant by nature.

Maintain your Griddle from Season to Season

There are some precautions you should take before putting away your griddle and using it again because you will likely keep it outside. Turn off the gas supply to the grill and close the valve before putting it away. An insect and dust-proof griddle cover is commercially available. Inspect the griddle's burner area for spider webs before using it again. Flare-ups can occur if spider webs are not removed prior to cooking. You should make sure you have enough gas in your tank before you begin cooking. The cooking surface should be reseasoned after the tank has been hooked up and before you begin cooking. If your griddle stops working, follow the steps above to get it working again.

The Best Method for Cleaning a Griddle

Your griddle should be cleaned after each use, but it should not be washed like regular pots and pans. You should avoid using dish soap to clean the cooking surface because you want to build up a great seasoning coating to protect your griddle and get the best results possible. The grease-cutting agent in most detergents will eat right through your seasoning coating. The best way to clean your griddle is to use a griddle scraper and hot water, just like the professionals do in restaurants. You can use a griddle scraper to remove any leftover food from the griddle without compromising the seasoning layer you've created. Most fats and sauces will dissolve in very hot water and can then be scraped away with a knife. While it is not necessary to season your grill after each cleaning, doing so regularly will keep your griddle dark and lustrous.

Invest in the Right Equipment

You'll need professional-grade cooking equipment to get the most out of your Gas Griddle. While you may have a variety of spatulas in your kitchen, investing in two long metal spatulas will help you get the most out of your griddle. These spatulas not only last a long time, but they also allow you to transport and turn a large amount of food at once. They're also thin and flexible, allowing you to scoop up heaping helpings of hash browns without spilling anything. A pair of long-handled metal tongs are also recommended because they allow you to reach everywhere on the griddle without getting burned.

Food Preparation is Essential

Make sure all of the necessary ingredients and raw foods are ready for the cook before beginning the actual cooking process. When you begin the actual cooking process, there is no time for chopping and cutting your ingredients, which increases the likelihood of food burning. So, before you begin cooking, always have your ingredients ready.

Experiment with Different Cooking Fats

Unlike a standard grill, which allows cooking fat to fall into the coals or gas jets, the Gas Griddle keeps cooking fat on your food! As a result, you can experiment with various types of cooking fat to achieve the best results. Diverse oils not only impart distinct flavors but also act in distinct ways. Olive oil adds a powerful and sometimes spicy black pepper flavor to meals. The problem with olive oil is that it has a low smoke point, which means that it begins to taste burned once it reaches a certain temperature. When cooking at a low to medium temperature, use olive oil; when cooking at a high temperature, avoid it. If you're looking for high-heat cooking oil, try canola or regular vegetable oil. They'll let you cook at high temperatures without getting a burnt flavor. Of course, butter has more flavor than almost anything else, but it also burns easily, so use it for low-heat cooking or quick-cooking meals.

When Cooking food, Use Basic Griddle Tools

Spatulas, scrapers, and squeeze bottles are some of the most fundamental griddle tools. While your meal is cooking on the griddle, you can use scrapers and spatulas to flip and mix the ingredients and squeeze bottles to add liquids like water, oil, and sausage.

Cook your Food with Additional Tools

A basting cover is included as an extra tool for steaming, roasting, and melting your food. Another useful tool is a grill press, which allows you to press your food while cooking to remove excess fat and oils.

When Cooking your Food, Use Water

The water will help your food cook faster. Squeeze a small amount of water over the hot griddle surface to create steam, which aids in the cooking of your food.

The Ideal Burger

For generations, people have been looking for the perfect burger. Since the invention of the hamburger, chefs have debated the best way to grind it, form the patties, and, of course, cook it. Some argue that imported Japanese waygu meat is required, while others argue that high heat over charcoal is the best method. So, we're putting an end to this feud once and for all. To make the best burger you've ever had, start by increasing the fat content. When you go shopping, you usually have the option of choosing between 20% fat and 10% fat. This is insufficient for the perfect burger. The ideal burger contains between 25 and 30% fat, and the simplest way to achieve this is to grind it yourself using a combination of chuck and short rib meat. If you don't want to do it yourself, tell your butcher that you need ground beef with more fat. Additionally, whenever possible, use fresh ground beef. The enemy of the perfect burger is compressed beef, and the longer it sits in packaging, the more compressed it becomes.

When you've found the right beef, shape it into 1/3-pound loose balls. You don't want to overwork it or squish the balls together; you want them to hold together. Set your griddle to medium heat and light the burners. High heat may appear to be the best way to cook burgers, but this is not the case. Allow plenty of time for the fat to render and produce a delicious sear on your burgers. If you overcook your burgers, they will be overcooked and chewy on the inside. Drizzle a little vegetable oil over the ball and place it on the griddle. Use a grill weight to flatten the burger as much as possible. Do not shape it; instead, place it on the griddle and season it with salt. Make an indentation in the center of the burger with your thumb to keep it flat. After the first side has formed a good sear, flip, season with salt, and cook for the same amount of time. While cooking this way, your burger will have more time to render fat and absorb it. Once you've reached the desired temperature, remove it from the griddle and set it aside for five minutes. Add your favorite toppings and enjoy the best burger you've ever had.

Outdoor Gas Griddle Temperature Chart

No.	Heat Levels	Temperature
1	Low	250 to 320°F
2	Medium	320 to 375°F
3	High	375 to 450°F or more

Conversion Tables of the Various Units of Measurement

CONVERSION CHART

Liquid Measure

8 ounces =	1 cup
2 cups =	1 pint
16 ounces =	1 pint
4 cups =	1 quart
1 gill =	1/2 cup or 1/4 pint
2 pints =	1 quart
4 quarts =	1 gallon
31.5 gal. =	1 barrel
3 tsp =	1 tbsp
2 tbsp =	1/8 cup or 1 fluid ounce
4 tbsp =	1/4 cup
8 tbsp =	1/2 cup
1 pinch =	1/8 tsp or less
1 tsp =	60 drops

Conversion of US Liquid Measure to Metric System

1 fluid oz. =	29.573 milliliters
1 cup =	230 milliliters
1 quart =	.94635 liters
1 gallon =	3.7854 liters
.033814 fluid ounce =	1 milliliter
3.3814 fluid ounces =	1 deciliter
33.814 fluid oz. or 1.0567 qt.=	1 liter

Dry Measure

2 pints =	1 quart
4 quarts =	1 gallon
8 quarts =	2 gallons or 1 peck
4 pecks =	8 gallons or 1 bushel
16 ounces =	1 pound
2000 lbs. =	1 ton

Conversion of US Weight and Mass Measure to Metric System

.0353 ounces =	1 gram
1/4 ounce =	7 grams
1 ounce =	28.35 grams
4 ounces =	113.4 grams
8 ounces =	226.8 grams
1 pound =	454 grams
2.2046 pounds =	1 kilogram
.98421 long ton or 1.1023 short tons =	1 metric ton

Linear Measure

12 inches =	1 foot
3 feet =	1 yard
5.5 yards =	1 rod
40 rods =	1 furlong
8 furlongs (5280 feet) =	1 mile
6080 feet =	1 nautical mile

Conversion of US Linear Measure to Metric System

1 inch =	2.54 centimeters
1 foot =	.3048 meters
1 yard =	.9144 meters
1 mile =	1609.3 meters or 1.6093 kilometers
.03937 in. =	1 millimeter
.3937 in.=	1 centimeter
3.937 in.=	1 decimeter
39.37 in.=	1 meter
3280.8 ft. or .62137 miles =	1 kilometer

To convert a Fahrenheit temperature to Centigrade, do the following:
a. Subtract 32   b. Multiply by 5   c. Divide by 9

To convert Centigrade to Fahrenheit, do the following:
a. Multiply by 9   b. Divide by 5   c. Add 32

Chapter 3: Breakfast Recipes

1. Breakfast Sandwich with Bacon and Swiss Cheese

(Preparation time: 10 minutes | Cooking time: 15 minutes | Servings: 2 | Difficulty: Easy)

Per serving: Calories 470, Total fat 21g, Protein 38g, Carbs 10g

Ingredients:

- 4 round rolls of sandwiches
- Salt and pepper to taste
- 4 tablespoons of ketchup
- 2 slices of bacon
- 4 tablespoons of Swiss grated cheese

Instructions:

- Begin by removing the sandwich tops.
- Using a spoon, remove the inside section of the sandwiches, being careful not to damage or split the crust.

- Use a small quantity of ketchup to fill each sandwich.
- Place the bacon, sliced into small pieces, on top of the tomato.
- Meanwhile, preheat your Griddle at 400°F for direct cooking.
- Brush olive oil on an oven-safe baking pan.
- Arrange the sandwiches into the pan as evenly as possible.
- Finish with a pinch of salt and pepper, then the shredded Swiss cheese.
- Put the pan on your griddle and cook for around 15 minutes on the griddle.
- Remove as soon as it's finished and serve immediately.

2. French Toast Sticks

(Preparation time: 10 minutes | Cooking time: 10 minutes | Servings: 2 | Difficulty: Easy)
Per serving: Calories 166, Total fat 7g, Protein 10g, Carbs 14g

Ingredients:

- 2 eggs
- 1 teaspoon of vanilla
- 2/3 cup of milk
- 4 bread slices, cut each bread slice into 3 pieces vertically
- 1/4 teaspoon of ground cinnamon

Instructions:

- Preheat your griddle at a low setting.
- Inside a mixing bowl, combine the eggs, cinnamon, vanilla, and milk.
- Coat the griddle's surface using cooking spray.
- Coat each slice of bread thoroughly in the egg mixture.
- Cook till both sides of the coated bread is golden brown on the hot griddle.
- Take pleasure in your food.

3. Porcini Mushrooms, Garlic and Bacon Omelet

(Preparation time: 10 minutes | Cooking time: 30 minutes | Servings: 4 | Difficulty: Easy)

Per serving: Calories 292, Total fat 14g, Protein 23g, Carbs 2g

Ingredients:

- 1 1/4 cups of porcini mushrooms, cleaned
- 1 garlic clove
- 5 eggs
- 4 teaspoons of olive oil
- 1 tablespoon of chives
- 1/2 cup of sliced bacon
- 1 pinch of salt

Instructions:

- To begin, clean and trim the chives.
- Garlic cloves should be peeled and washed as well.
- Before chopping the porcini mushrooms into 1/4-inch thin slices, clean them.
- Slice the bacon into thin strips.
- Inside a sauté pan over medium flame, sauté whole garlic clove and mushrooms in olive oil till tender.
- Cook for 1 minute after the bacon has been done.
- Remove the garlic clove.
- Remove the mushrooms from the flame and place them on a dry kitchen towel to cool.
- Meanwhile, preheat a zone of the griddle at 370°F and apply a layer of oil on griddle.
- Crack 3 eggs into a mixing bowl with the chives and whisk vigorously with a teaspoon of salt.
- Place the eggs on the hot griddle, followed by the garlic, bacon, and porcini mixture.
- Cook for about 15 minutes.
- To test for doneness, insert a knife into the center of your omelet; if the knife comes out clean, your omelet is ready to eat.

4. Sausage and Veggie Scramble

(Preparation time: 10 minutes | Cooking time: 20 minutes | Servings: 4 | Difficulty: Easy)

Per serving: Calories 342, Total fat 25g, Protein 23g, Carbs 6g

Ingredients:

- 1 green bell pepper, sliced
- 1/2 teaspoon of black pepper
- 1 teaspoon of salt
- 1/2 lb. of sausage, sliced into thin rounds or chopped
- 1 yellow onion, sliced
- 8 eggs, beaten
- Vegetable oil
- 1 cup of white mushrooms, sliced

Instructions:

- Preheat your griddle at medium/high temperature.
- Brush the griddle using vegetable oil before adding the peppers and mushrooms. Add the onions after a few minutes and sauté till they are lightly browned. Cook till the onions are soft, sprinkling with salt and pepper as needed.
- On the griddle, combine the sausage and veggies. Cook till they're lightly browned.
- Cook till the eggs are done to your satisfaction, then add them to the vegetables and mix them in. With a large spatula, remove the scramble off the griddle and serve immediately.

5. Avocado and Egg Breakfast Burrito

(Preparation time: 10 minutes | Cooking time: 10 minutes | Servings: 2 | Difficulty: Easy)

Per serving: Calories 683, Total fat 59g, Protein 38g, Carbs 48g

Ingredients:

- 1 small tomato, chopped
- 1 small bunch of fresh cilantro, chopped, or to taste
- 1 dash of hot sauce, or to taste
- 2 flour tortillas (10 inches)
- 1 cup of shredded mild cheddar cheese
- 1 Hass avocado - pitted, peeled, and sliced
- 4 medium eggs
- 1 pinch of salt and ground black pepper to taste
- 1 tablespoon of butter

Instructions:

- Preheat the griddle at medium temperature. Place the tortillas in a baking dish. Sprinkle shredded Cheddar cheese in the center of each tortilla, near the end. Melt the cheese by placing it on the griddle for around 20 to 30 seconds.
- Spread the butter on the griddle. Whisk the eggs together inside a mixing bowl. Place on the griddle and cook for 5 minutes or till the eggs are set.

- Scramble eggs over melted cheese on tortillas; top with avocado, tomato, and cilantro. Season using salt and pepper to taste. Finish with a splash of hot sauce.

6. Ricotta Cheese and Pistachio Sandwich

(Preparation time: 5 minutes | Cooking time: 15 minutes | Servings: 4 | Difficulty: Easy)

Per serving: Calories 250, Total fat 10g, Protein 19g, Carbs 18g

Ingredients:

- 4 tablespoons of pistachio cream
- 1/2 cup of ricotta cheese
- 8 slices of whole meal bread
- 6 tablespoons of melted butter

Instructions:

- Preheat the griddle at high temperature.
- Brush butter on both sides of the bread slices.
- Pistachio cream should be spread in the center of four slices.
- To make 4 sandwiches, brush 2 slices of bread with ricotta cheese and top with the remaining slices.
- Place the sandwiches on the griddle.
- Cook for around 10-12 minutes, checking to see if the cheese has completely melted.
- While still warm, cut and serve.

7. Oatmeal Breakfast Bars

(Preparation time: 15 minutes | Cooking time: 30 minutes | Servings: 8 | Difficulty: Easy)

Per serving: Calories 184, Total fat 7g, Protein 5g, Carbs 26g

Ingredients:

- 1 cup of milk
- ½ teaspoon of salt
- 2 eggs
- 1 tablespoon of white sugar
- ⅓ cup of packed brown sugar
- 1 teaspoon of vanilla extract

- ½ teaspoon of ground cinnamon
- 2 cups of old-fashioned rolled oats
- 1 ½ teaspoons of baking powder
- 2 tablespoons of canola oil

Instructions:

- Preheat the griddle at medium temperature. Grease an 8-inch square baking pan.
- Combine oats, brown sugar, salt, white sugar, baking powder, and cinnamon inside a mixing bowl. Whisk together the milk, canola oil, eggs, and vanilla extract in a separate bowl. Stir in the egg mixture till well combined; set aside for 20 minutes to enable flavors to mingle. Fill the prepared square pan halfway with the oats mixture.
- Cook on the griddle for about 30 minutes or until the edges are golden brown.

8. Egg White Breakfast Bites

(Preparation time: 15 minutes | Cooking time: 20 minutes | Servings: 12 | Difficulty: Easy)

Per serving: Calories 57, Total fat 3g, Protein 7g, Carbs 2g

Ingredients:

- 1 tablespoon of fresh basil, minced
- ¼ teaspoon of garlic powder
- ⅛ teaspoon of ground black pepper
- Cooking spray
- ¼ cup of crumbled feta cheese
- 1 carton of liquid egg whites (16 ounces)
- ¼ teaspoon of salt
- ½ cup of low-fat cottage cheese
- 1 cup of packed fresh spinach, finely chopped
- ⅓ cup of roasted red peppers, drained and chopped

Instructions:

- Preheat the griddle at medium temperature. Use nonstick cooking spray to coat a 12-cup muffin pan.
- Blend egg whites, salt, cottage cheese, garlic powder, and pepper inside a blender for 15 seconds, or till smooth.

- Combine the roasted red peppers, spinach, and basil inside a mixing dish. Pour in the egg mixture and thoroughly whisk it in. Fill each muffin cup 3/4 full with the mixture, which should be spooned evenly into the muffin cups. Top each muffin with 1 teaspoon of feta cheese.
- Place them on the griddle and cook for 18 to 20 minutes or till the egg bites are set.

9. Whole meal and Cocoa Pancake

(Preparation time: 15 minutes | Cooking time: 15 minutes | Servings: 4 | Difficulty: Easy)

Per serving: Calories 260, Total fat 5g, Protein 14g, Carbs 21g

Ingredients:

- 3 tablespoons of sugar
- ½ teaspoon of cinnamon
- 1 vanilla pod
- 3 eggs
- 1.5 cups of semi-skimmed milk
- 3/4 cup of whole meal flour
- 2 tablespoons of sugar-free cocoa
- Butter to taste
- 1 pinch of salt

Instructions:

- Scrape the vanilla seeds from the pod and keep the pod for later use.
- Combine the flour, salt, cocoa powder, sugar, vanilla seeds, and cinnamon inside a mixing bowl.
- Pour in the semi-skimmed milk and beer while stirring.
- Continue to mix while adding one egg at a time.
- When the batter has been fully blended, there should be no lumps. Refrigerate the batter for at least an hour.
- Preheat the griddle at medium-high.
- Spray the griddle top using cooking spray.
- Close the lid and for about 5 minutes to preheat it.
- Add the butter to the griddle and fry the pancakes one at a time, flipping once.

- Add more butter as needed.
- When the pancakes are done, fold them into triangles and cover them.
- Continue in this manner till all of the batter is gone.
- Serve and enjoy.

10. Charred Bread with Ricotta and Cherry Salsa

(Preparation time: 10 minutes | Cooking time: 10 minutes | Servings: 6 | Difficulty: Easy)

Per serving: Calories 177, Total fat 12g, Protein 6g, Carbs 13g

Ingredients:

- 12 ounces of fresh cherries, pitted & chopped into ⅓-inch-thick slivers
- Flaky sea salt, for garnish
- ½ cup of olive oil, plus more for the brushing
- 12 ounces of fresh ricotta (whole-milk)
- 5 tablespoons of fresh lemon juice
- 1 baguette, 1/2 lengthwise

Instructions:

- Inside a mixing dish, combine the lemon juice, cherries, and olive oil.
- Preheat the griddle at medium temperature.
- Spray the griddle top using cooking spray.
- The baguette's chopped edges should be oiled.
- Cook, cut sides down, for about 3 minutes, or till bread is golden brown and toasted.
- Allow the bread to cool for 1 minute before spreading generous quantity of ricotta on both pieces.
- Cut every half into six pieces on a diagonal.
- Arrange on a plate and top using cherry salsa.
- Serve with a dusting of sea salt.

11. Breakfast Burritos with Green Salsa

(Preparation time: 15 minutes | Cooking time: 25 minutes | Servings: 4 | Difficulty: Easy)

Per serving: Calories 721, Total fat 55g, Protein 35g, Carbs 56g

Ingredients:

- 8 small red potatoes, cut into 1/4 inch slices
- 1 tablespoon of chili powder
- ½ pound of bulk chorizo sausage
- 5 eggs, lightly beaten
- 1 package of cream cheese (4 ounces)
- 3 tablespoons of chopped fresh cilantro
- Salt and ground black pepper to taste
- ¼ cup of green salsa
- 2 tablespoons of olive oil
- 4 burrito size flour tortillas
- 1 tablespoon of butter

Instructions:

- Heat the griddle at medium-high temperature and coat using a thin layer of olive oil.
- Season the potato slices using salt, pepper, and chili powder and place them on top of the griddle. Cook for around 10 minutes or till the potatoes are tender. Remove from the griddle and place on a baking sheet, then return to the other side of the griddle at medium temperature.
- Cook the chorizo on the griddle, stirring frequently to break it apart, till it is browned and crumbly. Remove the chorizo from the griddle and arrange it on top of the potatoes on the griddle.
- Wrap the tortillas in aluminum foil and place them on the heated side of the griddle.
- Now place the skillet on the griddle; whisk the eggs continually while they cook. When the eggs are almost set, add the chorizo and potatoes. Stir in the cream cheese till fully melted, then mix in the cilantro just before serving.
- Place the eggs on the bottom half of each tortilla on separate plates. Fold the tortilla edges over the mixture; roll into a tight cylinder and serve with green salsa on top.

12. Breakfast English Muffin Strata

(Preparation time: 10 minutes | Cooking time: 40 minutes | Servings: 15 | Difficulty: Easy)

Per serving: Calories 359, Total fat 26g, Protein 18g, Carbs 13g

Ingredients:

- 1 package of English muffins, split (12 ounces)

- 8 large eggs
- 1 1/4 cups of sharp Cheddar cheese, shredded and divided
- 1 can of chopped green chilies, drained (4 ounces)
- 1 package of mozzarella cheese, shredded and divided (8 ounces)
- ¼ cup of butter, or as needed
- 1 package of ground pork sausage (16 ounces)
- 1 ½ cups of sour cream

Instructions:

- Heat the griddle at medium-high temperature and coat using a thin layer of olive oil.
- On the griddle, toss in the sausage. Cook for another 10 minutes or till the sausage is crumbled, equally browned, and no pinker.
- Lightly coat a 9x13-inch baking dish.
- A pat of butter should be placed inside of every English muffin half. Line a greased baking dish using buttered English muffins, then layer half of the sausage, half of the Cheddar cheese, and half of the mozzarella cheese on top.
- Inside a large-sized mixing bowl, whisk together the eggs, sour cream, & green chilies; pour over the sausage and cheese. Any leftover sausage, cheese, or mozzarella is sprinkled on top. Put in the fridge for at least 8 hours, covered.
- Transfer the dish to the griddle.
- Cook strata for 35 minutes or till lightly browned and hard in the center. Allow 10 minutes for rest before serving.

13. Mini Breakfast Quiches

(Preparation time: 10 minutes | Cooking time: 30 minutes | Servings: 12 | Difficulty: Easy)

Per serving: Calories 545, Total fat 37g, Protein 16g, Carbs 35g

Ingredients:

- 6 eggs
- 1 ½ cups of heavy cream
- 1 teaspoon of chili powder
- ½ cup of diced red bell pepper
- 2 cups of shredded Cheddar cheese
- ¼ cup of salsa
- ½ teaspoon of ground cumin
- 24 frozen mini tart shells (2 inches)
- ¼ cup of all-purpose flour
- 6 slices of bacon
- 2 teaspoons of onion powder
- ½ cup of diced green bell pepper
- 2 teaspoons of garlic salt
- ½ cup of cubed fully cooked ham

Instructions:

- Preheat the griddle at medium using a thin layer of oil on top. Place the tart shells in muffin cups and set aside.
- Cook the bacon on the griddle for about 10 minutes, occasionally stirring, till evenly browned. When cool, drain on a dish lined using paper towels and crumble.
- Inside a mixing bowl, whisk together the eggs, cream, flour, chili powder, garlic salt, onion powder, and cumin till smooth.
- Inside a mixing dish, combine the crumbled bacon, 2 cups of cheddar cheese, green and red bell peppers, ham, and salsa. Halfway fill the tart shells with the filling, then top with 1/2 cup of Cheddar cheese.
- Place the quiche on the griddle and cook for around 20 to 25 minutes, or till a knife inserted into the center comes out clean.

14. Fluffy Blueberry Pancakes

(Preparation time: 10 minutes | Cooking time: 10 minutes | Servings: 2 | Difficulty: Easy)

Per serving: Calories 499, Total fat 13g, Protein 16g, Carbs 46g

Ingredients:

- 3/4 cup of milk
- 2 tablespoons of sugar
- 1 teaspoon of baking powder
- 1/2 teaspoon of salt
- 2 tablespoons of butter, melted
- Butter for cooking
- 1 egg
- 2 tablespoons of white vinegar
- 1 cup of flour
- 1/2 teaspoon of baking soda
- 1 cup of fresh blueberries

Instructions:

- Inside a mixing bowl, combine the milk and vinegar. Allow two minutes for this to happen.
- Inside a large-sized mixing bowl, combine the flour, baking soda, sugar, baking powder, and salt. Combine the milk, blueberries, egg, and melted butter. Mix till the mixture is smooth but not totally creamy.
- Heat your griddle at medium temperature.
- Spray the griddle top using cooking spray.
- Cook the pancakes until golden brown on one side on the griddle. Cook till the other side of the pancakes is golden brown.
- Before serving, remove the pancakes from the griddle and drizzle using warm maple syrup.

15. Italian Egg, Sausage and Cheese Crunch Wrap

(Preparation time: 10 minutes | Cooking time: 15 minutes | Servings: 3 to 4 | Difficulty: Easy)

Per serving: Calories 286, Total fat 15g, Protein 12g, Carbs 26g

Ingredients:

- ½ cup of sharp cheddar cheese
- Large flour tortillas crispy
- 6 slices of American cheese
- Everything Bagel Seasoning
- 5 scrambled eggs
- Corn tortillas
- 3 hash browns
- Hot Italian sausage links, decased

Instructions:

- Spray the griddle top using cooking spray. Cook the decased sausage links till they have the consistency of ground meat on your Griddle over medium-high heat.
- Cook all hash browns in a large amount of butter, turning them over on both sides.
- Make the scrambled eggs to your liking.
- Warm the flour tortillas on the griddle for a few seconds before removing them.

- On a tortilla, top eggs with Everything Bagel Seasoning and cheese. Arrange a crispy corn tortilla on top of the cheese, followed by another layer of cheese and sausage. Fold the flour tortilla around the ingredients and top with the hash browns.

- To make the crunch wrap, start with the base of the flour tortilla and fold the upper edge over the center. As you make your way around, fold the flour tortilla over the center fillings.

- On the griddle, melt 1/4 cup of cheddar cheese. Then, fold the crunch wrap in half and place it on top of the cheese to form a crunchy cheddar seal. Flip the crispy wrap toast on the other side. Remove from the griddle and cut in half to serve.

16. Veggie Breakfast Cakes

(Preparation time: 10 minutes | Cooking time: 10 minutes | Servings: 2 | Difficulty: Easy)

Per serving: Calories 543, Total fat 24g, Protein 16g, Carbs 48g

Ingredients:

- 1 small tomato, diced
- 1 ¼ cups of biscuit baking mix
- 2 eggs
- ½ cup of chopped red bell pepper
- 1 teaspoon of chopped fresh parsley
- ½ cup of vanilla fat-free yogurt
- 1 tablespoon of vegetable oil
- ½ cup of chopped green bell pepper
- 1 onion, diced

Instructions:

- Whisk together the eggs, yogurt, and biscuit baking mix inside a medium-sized mixing bowl.
- Preheat the griddle at medium temperature.
- Spray the griddle top using cooking spray.
- Sauté the green bell pepper, onion, and red bell pepper till tender, then add it to the batter.
- Spoon the batter onto the griddle, roughly 1/4 cup for each pancake. Brown on all sides and serve immediately with parsley and tomatoes on the side.

17. Breakfast Potato Boats

(Preparation time: 15 minutes | Cooking time: 1-hour | Servings: 2 | Difficulty: Easy)

Per serving: Calories 575, Total fat 26g, Protein 21g, Carbs 45g

Ingredients:

- 2 tablespoons of butter, divided
- 1 slice of bacon
- 2 pinches of chopped fresh parsley, or to taste
- ⅓ cup of shredded cheddar cheese
- 2 eggs
- 1 teaspoon of chopped fresh parsley, or to taste
- 2 large potatoes
- Salt and ground black pepper to taste

Instructions:

- Apply a thin layer of oil to the griddle and preheat the griddle at medium temperature.
- After pricking the potatoes with a fork, place them on a griddle.
- Cook for about 40 minutes or till potatoes can be easily pierced with a fork.
- While the potatoes are cooking, brown the bacon on the other side of the griddle at medium-high heat for about 10 minutes, or till evenly browned.
- Using paper towels, drain the bacon. Allow for a 10-minute cooling period. Crumble.
- Remove the potatoes from the griddle and lay them aside for 10 minutes to cool.
- Cut the tops off the potatoes and scoop out the insides to make a deep bowl. Toss each potato with 1/2 tablespoon butter, 1 pinch of parsley, salt, and pepper to taste.
- An egg should be cracked into each potato. To each, add another 1/2 tablespoon of butter. Divide the bacon and cheddar cheese between the two potato servings.
- Return the potato to the griddle and cook for another 10 to 15 minutes or till the eggs are set. Sprinkle each with 1/2 teaspoon parsley.

18. Breakfast Enchiladas

(Preparation time: 15 minutes | Cooking time: 30 minutes | Servings: 8 | Difficulty: Easy)

Per serving: Calories 483, Total fat 25g, Protein 18g, Carbs 43g

Ingredients:

- 1 can of diced green chili peppers (4.5 ounces)
- 1 ½ cups of shredded cheddar cheese, divided
- 1 package of frozen hash brown potatoes (16 ounces)
- 8 flour tortillas (10 inches)
- 1 tablespoon of vegetable oil
- 1 cup of diced cooked ham
- 1 can of green chili enchilada sauce (28 ounces)

Instructions:

- Cook the hash browns and ham in 1 tablespoon oil inside a medium-sized skillet over medium flame. Combine 1/2 cup of Cheddar cheese and diced green chilies. Cook till the cheese has melted completely.
- Cover the bottom of a 9x13-inch baking dish with a tiny amount of enchilada sauce. After dipping each tortilla in the leftover sauce, fill it with the potato-ham combination. Roll each one tightly and place the seam side down in the baking dish. Wrap in tin foil and top with the remaining sauce and cheese.
- Lightly coat a griddle using cooking spray or oil. Preheat the griddle for 10 minutes at medium temperature.
- Cook, covered, for around 20 minutes. Remove the foil and cook for an additional 10 minutes or till the top is lightly browned. Serve immediately.

19. Gorgonzola and Figs Toast

(Preparation time: 10 minutes | Cooking time: 10 minutes | Servings: 6 | Difficulty: Easy)

Per serving: Calories 370, Total fat 8g, Protein 15g, Carbs 39g

Ingredients:

- 1 baguette (or other bread you like more)
- ¼ of a teaspoon of salt
- 1 tablespoon of olive oil
- 6 big figs
- 1/2 cup of crumbled gorgonzola

- 1 teaspoon of balsamic vinegar
- ½ teaspoon of black pepper

Instructions:

- Preheat the griddle at medium temperature.
- Spray the griddle top using cooking spray.
- Meanwhile, cut the bread into 12 long, thin slices.
- Rinse and pat dry the figs after cleaning them.
- Clip and trim any overgrown stem ends.
- Inside a medium-sized mixing bowl, combine the figs, vinegar, pepper, and salt.
- Allow the figs to sit at room temperature for at least 15 minutes or up to 1 hour in the refrigerator, covered, to allow flavors to blend.
- Place the bread slices on the griddle and brush using olive oil.
- Toast them for 7 minutes on the griddle, flipping once, till they are lightly toasted.
- When you're ready to serve, taste the fig mixture and season to taste.
- Place one tablespoon of gorgonzola on each baguette slice, followed by an equal amount of fig mixture.

20. Hearty Breakfast Muffins

(Preparation time: 10 minutes | Cooking time: 20 minutes | Servings: 12 | Difficulty: Easy)

Per serving: Calories 227, Total fat 10g, Protein 4g, Carbs 32g

Ingredients:

- 1 cup of whole wheat flour
- 2 carrots, shredded
- ½ cup of packed brown sugar
- ½ cup of rolled oats
- 2 bananas, mashed
- ½ cup of shredded coconut
- 1 teaspoon of ground cinnamon
- ½ teaspoon of ground ginger
- 2 eggs

- ¼ cup of vegetable oil
- 1 zucchini, shredded
- ½ cup of dried cherries
- 1 ½ teaspoons of baking soda
- ½ cup of chopped pecans
- 1 teaspoon of salt
- ¼ cup of yogurt

Instructions:

- Preheat the griddle at medium temperature. Place on it 12 muffin cups, lightly oiled or lined using paper liners.
- Inside a large-sized mixing dish, combine carrots, bananas, yogurt, zucchini, vegetable oil, and eggs.
- Inside a separate bowl, whisk together the flour and baking soda. The flour combination should include brown sugar, nuts, oats, coconut, salt, cherries, cinnamon, and ginger. In a mixing bowl, combine wet and dry ingredients and stir till just combined.
- Fill the prepared muffin cups halfway with the batter.
- Cook till a toothpick inserted into the center of a muffin comes out clean, and the sides are slightly brown, about 17 to 22 minutes on the griddle. Allow cooling for about 10 minutes in the pans before transferring them to a wire rack to cool completely.

Chapter 4: Burger Recipes

1. Barbecue Cheese Burgers

(Preparation time: 10 minutes | Cooking time: 15 minutes | Servings: 6 | Difficulty: Easy)

Per serving: Calories 236, Total fat 15g, Protein 19g, Carbs 15g

Ingredients:

- ½ cup of mesquite-flavored barbecue sauce
- 2 cloves of garlic, minced
- ½ teaspoon of coarsely ground black pepper
- 1 cup of grated Monterey Jack or extra-sharp cheddar cheese
- ½ small red onion halved and thinly sliced
- 3 pounds of ground beef sirloin
- ½ teaspoon of curry powder
- 1 tablespoon of chili powder

- ½ teaspoon of salt

Instructions:

- Inside a large-sized mixing bowl, combine all of the ingredients except the cheese and onion till well combined. Make 6 patties, about 1 inch thick each.
- Preheat the griddle at medium-high and brush it using olive oil.
- Cook the burgers on the heated griddle till done to your liking, roughly 5 minutes per side. Top with cheese and onion for the last minute of cooking.
- It goes well with toasted sesame seed burger buns or onion rolls.
- Finish with lettuce and tomato slices.

2. Italian Hamburgers

(Preparation time: 10 minutes | Cooking time: 20 minutes | Servings: 6 | Difficulty: Easy)

Per serving: Calories 684, Total fat 28g, Protein 41g, Carbs 65g

Ingredients:

- 1/2 cup of Italian-flavored dry bread crumbs
- 6 hamburger buns, split
- 0.7-oz. pkg. of Italian salad dressing mix
- 2 eggs, beaten
- 1 1/2 lbs. of ground beef
- 2 slices of bacon, crisply cooked and crumbled
- 1 cup of shredded mozzarella cheese

Instructions:

- Inside a large-sized mixing bowl, combine all of the ingredients (except the buns). Mix well and divide into 6 patties.
- Preheat the griddle to medium-high heat and brush it with a thin layer of olive oil.
- Cook for 5 to 8 minutes on each side on the griddle till the desired amount of doneness is obtained. Serve on toasted buns.

3. Asian Turkey Burgers

(Preparation time: 10 minutes | Cooking time: 20 minutes | Servings: 4 | Difficulty: Easy)

Per serving: Calories 197, Total fat 10g, Protein 23g, Carbs 15g

Ingredients:

- 1½ tablespoons of toasted sesame oil (see Note)
- 6 cloves of garlic, minced
- 1 tablespoon of peeled & minced fresh ginger
- ¼ cup of finely chopped fresh cilantro leaves
- 1¾ pounds of ground turkey
- ¼ cup of soy sauce

Instructions:

- Gently incorporate all of the ingredients inside a large-sized mixing bowl using your hands. Make four 1-inch thick patties.
- Preheat your griddle at medium-high heat and brush it with a thin layer of olive oil.
- Cook the patties for 5 to 8 minutes on each side on the griddle.
- Serve with toasted sesame seeds on sesame seed buns. On top, drizzle with wasabi mayo or orange snow pea salad.

4. Cuban Frita Burgers

(Preparation time: 10 minutes | Cooking time: 15 minutes | Servings: 4 | Difficulty: Easy)

Per serving: Calories 101, Total fat 6g, Protein 8g, Carbs 4g

Ingredients:

- 2 teaspoons of ketchup
- 1 pound of ground beef round
- 1 teaspoon of salt
- ½ cup of plain dry bread crumbs
- 2 cloves of garlic, minced
- ½ teaspoon of ground cumin
- 1 large of egg
- ½ teaspoon of dried oregano
- 1 small onion, finely chopped
- ½ teaspoon of coarsely ground black pepper
- 1 teaspoon of sweet paprika

- ¼ cup of milk

Instructions:

- Set aside the bread crumbs and milk inside a small-sized mixing bowl.
- Gently combine the meat, half of the onion, the egg, salt, garlic, ketchup, paprika, cumin, pepper, and oregano inside a medium-sized mixing bowl. After folding in the breadcrumb mixture, thoroughly combine. Make 8 patties that are about 1/2 inch thick.
- Preheat the griddle to medium-high heat and brush it using olive oil.
- Cook the burgers till done to your taste on the heated griddle, about 2 to 4 minutes per side for medium.
- Serve with dinner rolls. Finish with the remaining chopped onion and potato sticks.

5. German Burgers

(Preparation time: 10 minutes | Cooking time: 20 minutes | Servings: 6 | Difficulty: Easy)

Per serving: Calories 358, Total fat 21g, Protein 12g, Carbs 31g

Ingredients:

- 14-1/2 oz. can of sauerkraut, drained
- 1/2 teaspoon of caraway seed
- 6 pumpernickel sandwich buns, split
- 1/8 teaspoon of pepper
- 2 tablespoons of beer or beef broth
- 1-1/2 lbs. of ground beef
- For garnish: additional mustard
- 6 slices of Swiss cheese
- 1/2 cup of soft pumpernickel bread crumbs
- 1 teaspoon of mustard
- 1/2 teaspoon of salt

Instructions:

- Inside a large-sized mixing dish, combine all ingredients except the cheese, buns, and sauerkraut. Combine all ingredients gently and shape into 6 patties.
- Preheat the griddle at medium-high heat and brush it using a thin layer of olive oil.

- Cook the patties on the griddle for around 10 to 15 minutes, flipping halfway through or till done to preference. Place the cheese on top and set aside till it melts. Grill the buns, if desired. Burgers should be served with sauerkraut and mustard on top of buns.

6. Middle Eastern Turkey Kibbeh Burgers

(Preparation time: 10 minutes | Cooking time: 30 minutes | Servings: 8 | Difficulty: Easy)

Per serving: Calories 359, Total fat 19g, Protein 29g, Carbs 17g

Ingredients:

- ½ pound of ground turkey
- 1 medium-sized yellow onion, finely chopped
- ½ cup of pine nuts
- ½ teaspoon of salt
- 1 tablespoon of olive oil
- ½ teaspoon of ground cinnamon
- 1 pound of sweet Italian turkey sausage, casings removed
- ½ cup of chicken broth
- Grated zest of 1 orange
- ½ cup of fine-grind bulgur wheat
- ½ teaspoon of ground coriander

Instructions:

- Preheat the griddle at medium-high heat.
- Heat the oil inside a medium-sized pan on the griddle. Cook, stirring regularly, till the onion is translucent, about 1 minute.
- Remove the pan from the griddle and add the pine nuts. Place them aside.
- Inside a large-sized mixing bowl, combine the bulgur, 1/4 cup chicken broth, the zest, cinnamon, coriander, and salt. Combine the ground turkey and the remaining 1/4 cup of broth.
- With the back of a tablespoon, spread the sausage into a 9 x 14-inch baking pan. Cover the entire bottom of the pan, filling in the corners and ensuring no gaps. Distribute the onion mixture evenly over the meat. With your hands, spread the bulgur-turkey mixture on top. Cook for around 30 minutes on the griddle or till a lovely crust forms.

- Using a serrated knife and a metal spatula, cut the mixture into 8 rectangular burgers.
- In the Cucumber Mint Sauce, replace the garlic with 1/4 cup of finely sliced red onion. Remove the top layer from each burger, then apply the sauce on top before replacing the top layer.

7. Spicy Tofu and Pork Burgers

(Preparation time: 10 minutes | Cooking time: 20 minutes | Servings: 6 | Difficulty: Easy)

Per serving: Calories 310, Total fat 10g, Protein 14g, Carbs 19g

Ingredients:

- 1 12-ounce package of firm tofu, drained
- ¾ teaspoon of salt
- 2 teaspoons of Asian chili garlic sauce
- ½ teaspoon of toasted sesame oil
- 1 pound of ground pork
- ½ teaspoon of cornstarch
- 1 large egg, lightly beaten
- ½ teaspoon of sugar
- 1 scallion (white & green parts), minced
- ¼ teaspoon of ground white pepper

Instructions:

- Inside a large-sized mixing bowl, combine the pork, chili garlic sauce, 1/4 teaspoon salt, 1/4 teaspoon sugar, and cornstarch. Place them aside.
- Mash the tofu inside a large-sized mixing bowl, then cover it in double-thickness cheesecloth. Twist the ends together to squeeze out as much liquid as possible. Repeat the process two more times. Scoop out the tofu and mix in the remaining 1/2 teaspoon salt, 1/4 teaspoon sugar, sesame oil, egg, white pepper, and scallions. Before adding to the pork mixture and mixing again, completely combine all ingredients. Form the mixture into 6 1-inch-thick patties.
- Preheat your griddle at medium-high heat and brush it with a thin layer of olive oil.
- Cook the patties for around 8 to 10 minutes per side on the griddle or till done to your preference.
- Serve on burger buns with chili garlic sauce.

8. Open-Faced Lone Star Burgers

(Preparation time: 10 minutes | Cooking time: 20 minutes | Servings: 6 | Difficulty: Easy)

Per serving: Calories 464, Total fat 29g, Protein 30g, Carbs 20g

Ingredients:

- 6 slices of frozen garlic Texas toast
- 1 tablespoon of brown sugar, packed
- 1-1/2 cup of shredded Colby Jack cheese, divided
- 2 cloves of garlic, minced
- 1/4 teaspoon of dried thyme
- 1 teaspoon of steak sauce
- 1/4 cup of onion, chopped
- 8-oz. can of tomato sauce
- 1-1/2 lbs. of ground beef
- 1 teaspoon of Worcestershire sauce

Instructions:

- Inside a large-sized mixing dish, combine the onion, garlic, thyme, and one cup of cheese. Toss in the crumbled beef and mix. Form the mixture into 6 oval-shaped patties.
- Preheat your griddle at medium-high heat and brush it using a thin layer of olive oil.
- Cook the patties on the griddle for 5 to 10 minutes per side or till done to your preference. Place on the buns to serve.
- Meanwhile, make the toast according to the package directions. Drain the burgers and keep them warm.
- Toss the remaining ingredients into the pan on the griddle. Bring to the boil, then simmer, stirring frequently, for 2 minutes or till slightly thickened. Return the burgers to the pan and turn them over to coat. On top, sprinkle with the remaining cheese. Burgers should be served with toast.

9. Key West Burgers

(Preparation time: 10 minutes | Cooking time: 20 minutes | Servings: 4 | Difficulty: Easy)

Per serving: Calories 611, Total fat 48g, Protein 49g, Carbs 45g

Ingredients:

- 1 lb. of ground beef
- Salt and pepper to taste
- Hamburger buns, split and toasted
- 3 tablespoons of Key lime juice
- 1/4 cup of fresh cilantro, chopped
- For garnish: lettuce

For the Creamy Burger Spread:

- 1 cup of sour cream
- 3 green onion tops, chopped
- 1 cup of cream cheese softened

Instructions:

- Inside a mixing bowl, combine the meat, lime juice, salt, cilantro, and pepper. Form the beef mixture into four patties.
- Preheat your griddle at medium-high heat and brush it using a thin layer of olive oil.
- Mix up all of the burger spread ingredients till well blended. After covering, place in the refrigerator for at least 15 minutes.
- After turning the burgers, cook the patties on the griddle for about 6 minutes. On the bottom halves of the buns, top with patties and lettuce. Creamy Burger is a fantastic addition. Spread the spread on the tops of the buns to close the sandwiches.

10. Crunchy Chicken Burgers

(Preparation time: 10 minutes | Cooking time: 20 minutes | Servings: 4 to 6 | Difficulty: Easy)

Per serving: Calories 566, Total fat 28g, Protein 41g, Carbs 38g

Ingredients:

- 4 to 6 hamburger buns, split
- 1/4 cup of honey barbecue sauce
- 1 lb. of ground chicken
- 3/4 cup of mini shredded wheat cereal, crushed
- 1 egg, beaten
- 1/8 teaspoon of salt

- 1/8 teaspoon of pepper

Instructions:

- Except for the buns, combine the ingredients and shape them into 4 to 6 patties.
- Preheat the griddle at medium-high heat and brush it using a thin layer of olive oil.
- Cook for around 5 to 10 minutes per side or till the center is no longer pink. Serve on buns with your favorite sauces and toppings.

11. Mexican Burgers

(Preparation time: 10 minutes | Cooking time: 20 minutes | Servings: 5 | Difficulty: Easy)

Per serving: Calories 536, Total fat 24g, Protein 48g, Carbs 33g

Ingredients:

- 1-1/4 lbs. of ground beef
- 2 chopped green onions
- 1 avocado, pitted, peeled & diced
- 1 beaten egg
- 1/2 teaspoon of chili powder
- 1 plum tomato, diced
- 1-1/4 cup of shredded Pepper Jack cheese
- 3/4 cup to 1 cup of tortilla chips nacho-flavored, crushed
- 1 to 2 teaspoons of lime juice
- Salt and pepper to taste
- 1/4 cup of fresh cilantro, chopped
- 5 hamburger buns, split
- 1/2 teaspoon of ground cumin

Instructions:

- Mash the avocado, onions, tomato, and lime juice together and set aside. Combine the meat, chips, egg, and seasonings inside a large-sized mixing dish. Make 5 patties out of the mixture.
- Preheat the griddle at the medium-high flame and brush it using a thin layer of olive oil.

- Cook for around 4 to 5 minutes per side on the griddle or till done to preference. Add the cheese to the burgers and cook till the cheese has melted. Serve with the avocado mixture slathered on top of the buns.

12. Grilled Summer Burgers

(Preparation time: 10 minutes | Cooking time: 20 minutes | Servings: 4 | Difficulty: Easy)

Per serving: Calories 376, Total fat 18g, Protein 26g, Carbs 25g

Ingredients:

- 1 teaspoon of salt
- 2 tablespoons of green pepper, finely chopped
- 1 lb. of ground beef
- 2 teaspoons of mustard
- 1/2 cup of onion, chopped
- 4 to 5 hamburger buns, split
- 1-1/2 tablespoons of prepared horseradish
- 3 tablespoons of catsup
- Pepper to taste

Instructions:

- Inside a mixing bowl, combine all ingredients except the buns. Form the mixture into patties.
- Preheat your griddle at medium-high heat and brush it using a thin layer of olive oil.
- Cook for 5 to 8 minutes on each side or till done to your satisfaction. Place on the buns to serve.

13. Smoked Trout Burgers with Horseradish and Ricotta

(Preparation time: 10 minutes | Cooking time: 20 minutes | Servings: 6 | Difficulty: Easy)

Per serving: Calories 390, Total fat 24g, Protein 40g, Carbs 13g

Ingredients:

- ½ pound of smoked trout, cut into small chunks
- 3 tablespoons of prepared horseradish
- ½ cup of ricotta cheese (fat-free works well)

Instructions:

- Inside a food processor, combine the trout, horseradish, and ricotta and pulse to combine.
- Continue mixing inside a medium-sized mixing bowl till all of the ingredients are thoroughly incorporated. Make six 1/2-inch-thick patties.
- Preheat your griddle at medium-high heat and brush it using a thin layer of olive oil.
- Cook the patties for 5 to 10 minutes on each side or till they are opaque all the way through.
- Serve on burger buns with finely cut green apple and thin red onion slices on top.

14. Tex-Mex Burgers

(Preparation time: 10 minutes | Cooking time: 20 minutes | Servings: 8 | Difficulty: Easy)

Per serving: Calories 614, Total fat 49g, Protein 38g, Carbs 28g

Ingredients:

- 2 lbs. of ground beef
- 1 cup of shredded Cheddar cheese
- 1/2 cup of salsa
- 2 to 3 cups of tortilla chips, crushed
- 1/2 cup of onion, grated
- 8 sandwich buns, split

Instructions:

- Inside a mixing bowl, combine all ingredients (excluding the buns) and shape them into patties.
- Preheat the griddle at medium-high heat and brush it using a thin layer of olive oil.
- Cook the patties on the griddle for 5 to 10 minutes on each side, flipping once, till done to your preference. Serve on toasted buns.

15. Bulgarian Burgers

(Preparation time: 10 minutes | Cooking time: 20 minutes | Servings: 4 | Difficulty: Easy)

Per serving: Calories 690, Total fat 45g, Protein 52g, Carbs 20g

Ingredients:

- 3 tablespoons of minced fresh flat-leaf parsley leaves
- 1 small onion, minced

- 1 teaspoon of salt
- 8 ounces of ground pork
- ½ teaspoon of ground cumin
- 8 ounces of ground veal
- ½ teaspoon of ground black pepper

Instructions:

- Combine all of the ingredients inside a large-sized mixing bowl and stir gently using a wooden spoon. Season the mixture by sautéing a small portion inside a nonstick skillet till cooked through. Season using salt and pepper to taste, and adjust seasonings as needed; the mixture should be well seasoned.
- Divide the meat into four equal portions. Wet your hands lightly using cold water before shaping each component into a 3/4-inch thick patty.
- Preheat the griddle at medium-high heat and brush it using a thin layer of olive oil.
- Cook the patties on the griddle for around 5 to 10 minutes on each side or till done to preference.
- Serve it over flaky toasted buns or country bread with feta salad on the side.

16. Seekh Kebab Burgers

(Preparation time: 10 minutes | Cooking time: 20 minutes | Servings: 4 | Difficulty: Easy)

Per serving: Calories 512, Total fat 34g, Protein 16g, Carbs 36g

Ingredients:

- 2 cloves of garlic, minced
- 1 tablespoon of minced fresh cilantro leaves
- ½ teaspoon of coarsely ground black pepper
- 1 teaspoon of sweet paprika
- ½ teaspoon of garam masala
- 1 pound of ground lamb
- ¼ cup of plain dry bread crumbs
- 1 teaspoon of ground cumin
- ¾ teaspoon of ground ginger
- 1 teaspoon of salt

- 1 teaspoon of ground coriander
- ½ teaspoon of turmeric
- 1 large egg
- 2 tablespoons of canola oil

Instructions:

- Inside a medium-sized mixing bowl, gently combine all of the ingredients except the oil. Cover using plastic wrap and chill for at least 30 minutes to enable the flavors to emerge.
- Form the mixture into four 1/2-inch thick patties.
- Preheat your griddle at medium-high heat and brush it using a thin layer of olive oil.
- Cook the patties for around 6 to 8 minutes per side on the griddle or till done to your preference.
- Finish with smashed onion and fresh cilantro on the burger buns.

17. Asian Salmon Burgers

(Preparation time: 10 minutes | Cooking time: 20 minutes | Servings: 4 | Difficulty: Easy)

Per serving: Calories 236, Total fat 15g, Protein 20g, Carbs 15g

Ingredients:

- 1 pound of salmon fillets, skin & any bones removed
- 1 small onion, grated
- 2½ tablespoons of Chinese oyster sauce

Instructions:

- Inside a food processor, pulse the salmon till it resembles a coarse paste. Pulse to combine the onion and oyster sauce. Transfer to a medium-sized mixing bowl, cover in plastic wrap and freeze for at least 30 minutes to firm up. Make four 1/2-inch thick patties.
- Preheat your griddle at medium-high heat and brush it using a thin layer of olive oil.
- Cook the patties for 5 to 8 minutes on each side or till they are opaque all the way through.
- Finish with lemon juice, a dash of oyster sauce, and thinly sliced red onion atop the brioche buns.

18. Bacon-Gouda Burgers

(Preparation time: 10 minutes | Cooking time: 20 minutes | Servings: 4 | Difficulty: Easy)

Per serving: Calories 553, Total fat 22g, Protein 46g, Carbs 47g

Ingredients:

- 1-1/2 lbs. of ground beef sirloin
- 1-3/4 cup of onion, thinly sliced
- 1 teaspoon of the hot pepper sauce
- 4 slices of smoked Gouda cheese
- 1/4 cup of finely chopped onion
- 6 slices of bacon, sliced into 1/2-inch chunks, cooked crisply, & 1 tablespoon of reserved drippings
- 2 tablespoons of olive oil
- Optional: crisply cooked lettuce leaves, bacon, sliced tomato
- 1/4 cup of steak sauce
- 2 teaspoons of Worcestershire sauce
- 4 onion rolls or kaiser rolls, split & toasted
- 1 tablespoon of steak seasoning

Instructions:

- Preheat the griddle at medium-high heat.
- Spray the griddle top using cooking spray.
- Cook the bacon on the griddle for about 4 to 5 minutes; now add the onion and cook for yet another 2 to 3 minutes. Place the bacon and onion inside a small-sized bowl and set aside. Now heat the oil on the griddle; add the onion and cook, covered, for about ten minutes or till golden. Place in a separate bowl with the steak sauce and set aside.
- Inside a large-sized mixing bowl, combine the meat, remaining sauces, seasonings, and onion-bacon combination; mix lightly and shape into four patties. Apply a little layer of olive oil to it.
- Cook for around 8 to 10 minutes on each side, or till done to preference, then top with mozzarella slices when almost done. On toasted bread, top burgers with the sliced onion mixture and any other desired toppings.

19. Chicken Marsala Burgers

(Preparation time: 10 minutes | Cooking time: 20 minutes | Servings: 6 | Difficulty: Easy)

Per serving: Calories 448, Total fat 27g, Protein 29g, Carbs 23g

Ingredients:

- 2 pounds of ground chicken
- 1 cup of chicken broth
- ¼ cup plus 2 tablespoons of dry Marsala
- 2 tablespoons of finely chopped fresh flat-leaf parsley leaves
- ½ teaspoon of all-purpose flour
- 2 tablespoons of minced shallots
- ¼ teaspoon of salt
- 1 tablespoon of olive oil
- ⅛ teaspoon of coarsely ground black pepper
- 10 ounces of white mushrooms, thinly sliced

Instructions:

- Inside a small-sized bowl, make a slurry with the flour and 1/2 cup of the broth. Place them aside.
- Preheat the griddle at medium-high heat.
- Place a big pan on the griddle. Cook for 1 minute or till the shallots are clear. To combine, whisk in the mushrooms and shallots. Cook for 5 minutes more after adding 1/4 cup broth. Cook for 10 to 15 minutes, or till the liquid has been reduced by three-quarters, before adding 1/4 cup Marsala, salt, and pepper. Stir in the parsley and slurry to the mixture after transferring the mixture inside a medium-sized mixing dish.
- Inside a mixing bowl, combine the remaining 2 tablespoons of Marsala with the ground chicken. Form the mixture into 6 1-inch-thick patties. Cook for around 15 minutes, flipping often, in the same pan with the burgers and the remaining 1/4 cup broth.
- After adding the mushroom mixture to the pan, cook for another 5 minutes.
- It goes well with toasted sesame seed buns. Finally, top with a mushroom mixture.

20. Bean & Chile Burgers

(Preparation time: 10 minutes | Cooking time: 20 minutes | Servings: 4 | Difficulty: Easy)

Per serving: Calories 433, Total fat 27g, Protein 13g, Carbs 36g

Ingredients:

- 1 cup of cooked rice
- 4-oz. can of green chilies
- 1/4 teaspoon of garlic powder
- 16-oz. can of black beans, drained and rinsed
- 1 teaspoon of onion powder
- 4 sandwich buns, split
- 11-oz. can of corn, drained
- salt to taste
- 1/2 cup of cornmeal
- Optional: salsa

Instructions:

- Preheat the griddle at medium-high heat and brush it using a thin layer of olive oil.
- Mash the beans inside a large-sized mixing bowl, then add the corn, onion powder, chilies, rice, cornmeal, and garlic powder. Season the ingredients and shape them into four large patties. Cook the patties on the griddle till golden brown on both sides, about 4 to 5 minutes per side. If preferred, serve on buns with salsa on the side.

Chapter 5: Vegetarian and Side Dish Recipes

1. Creamy Grilled Potato Salad

(Preparation time: 15 minutes | Cooking time: 10 minutes | Servings: 8 | Difficulty: Easy)

Per serving: Calories 132, Total fat 9g, Protein 2g, Carbs 14g

Ingredients:

- 2 (1.5 lbs.) bags of baby white potatoes

For the dressing:

- 1 teaspoon of celery seed
- 2 teaspoons of apple cider vinegar
- 1 tablespoon of Dijon mustard
- 1 tablespoon of fresh basil, chopped
- ½ teaspoon of sea salt
- 1 tablespoon of lemon juice

- ½ cup of mayonnaise
- 1 tablespoon of sour cream
- 2 tablespoons of olive oil
- ½ teaspoon of black pepper
- 1 tablespoon of fresh parsley, chopped

Instructions:

- Preheat the griddle using a thin layer of olive oil at medium-high heat.
- Cook the potatoes on the griddle for around 10 minutes or till cooked.
- Remove the potatoes out from the griddle and set them aside to cool for 10 minutes.
- Whisk together the dressing ingredients inside a large-sized mixing dish till well combined.
- Fold in the potatoes till well blended before serving at room temperature or chilled overnight.

2. Easy Fried Rice

(Preparation time: 10 minutes | Cooking time: 10 minutes | Servings: 2 | Difficulty: Easy)

Per serving: Calories 557, Total fat 20g, Protein 14g, Carbs 49g

Ingredients:

- 2 tablespoons of olive oil
- 2 tablespoons of green onion, sliced
- 4 cups of rice, cooked
- 1 teaspoon of salt
- 2 large eggs

Instructions:

- Set aside the eggs inside a mixing dish.
- Preheat your griddle at medium-high heat.
- Coat the griddle's top using cooking spray.
- On a hot griddle, cook the rice till it separates.
- Push rice to one side of the griddle top. Pour the beaten egg over the hot griddle.
- Cook till the rice grains are thoroughly covered by the egg.

- 2 minutes later, add the green onion.
- Serve and enjoy.

3. Spinach Salad with Tomato Melts

(Preparation time: 10 minutes | Cooking time: 10 minutes | Servings: 4 | Difficulty: Easy)

Per serving: Calories 121, Total fat 15g, Protein 8g, Carbs 17g

Ingredients:

- 3 cups of baby spinach
- 1 teaspoon of Dijon mustard
- 2 tablespoons of good-quality olive oil, plus more for brushing
- 1 or 2 large fresh tomatoes (enough for 4 thick slices across)
- 6 slices of cheddar cheese (about 4 ounces)
- 2 teaspoons of white wine vinegar
- Salt and pepper

Instructions:

- After you've cored the tomatoes, save the trimmings and cut 4 thick slices (approximately 1 inch). Brush both sides using oil and sprinkle with salt and pepper.
- Combine the 2 tablespoons of oil, vinegar, and mustard inside a mixing bowl. Toss the tomato trimmings with the spinach in the dressing till everything is evenly coated.
- Preheat your griddle at medium-high heat. Allow the griddle to heat till the oil shimmers but does not smoke. Cook the tomato slices for around 3 minutes.
- Cook for another 2 to 3 minutes, or till the cheese is melted, after flipping the tomatoes.
- Serve with the salad on top of the dishes.

4. Green Beans in Mustard Sauce

(Preparation time: 10 minutes | Cooking time: 10 minutes | Servings: 4 | Difficulty: Easy)

Per serving: Calories 70, Total fat 2g, Protein 4g, Carbs 8g

Ingredients:

- 1 tablespoon of smoked paprika
- 2 tablespoons of olive oil
- Salt and pepper to taste

- 2 lbs. of green beans, fresh

For the sauce:

- 1 teaspoon of mayonnaise
- 1 teaspoon of olive oil
- Salt and pepper to taste
- 1 teaspoon of yellow mustard
- 1/2 cup of white yogurt
- 1 teaspoon of onion powder

Instructions:

- Green beans should be cleaned and dried beforehand.
- Toss fresh green beans in seasoned olive oil and paprika till uniformly coated.
- Preheat the griddle at a high temperature.
- Spray the griddle top using cooking spray.
- Toss in the green beans every few minutes.
- Sprinkle with salt & pepper to taste. Cook till the green beans are done to your liking.
- Meanwhile, whisk together all of the sauce ingredients inside a mixing bowl.
- When the green beans are thoroughly cooked, remove them from the griddle and leave them aside for a few minutes.
- Serve the green beans with the mustard sauce on individual serving plates.

5. Roasted Broccoli with Parmesan

(Preparation time: 10 minutes | Cooking time: 20 minutes | Servings: 6 | Difficulty: Easy)

Per serving: Calories 85, Total fat 5g, Protein 6g, Carbs 7g

Ingredients:

- 1/4 teaspoon of pepper
- 2 tablespoons of lemon juice
- 1 clove of minced garlic
- 6 cups of fresh broccoli, cut into bite-sized chunks
- 1/4 cup of grated Parmesan cheese
- 2 tablespoons of olive oil
- 1/4 teaspoon of salt

Instructions:

- Fill a large-sized resealable bag halfway using broccoli.
- Combine the broccoli, lemon juice, salt, oil, garlic, and pepper inside a mixing bowl. Allow for a 30-minute break.

- Preheat the griddle at medium temperature.
- Spray the griddle top using cooking spray.
- To keep the broccoli from sticking to the griddle, place it in a grilling basket or on a sheet tray. Cook for 8 to 10 minutes on the griddle or until crisp but tender. Remove from the griddle and top with Parmesan. Enjoy!

6. Tofu Skewers with Spicy Peanut Sauce

(Preparation time: 15 minutes | Cooking time: 15 minutes | Servings: 8 | Difficulty: Easy)

Per serving: Calories 138, Total fat 11g, Protein 6g, Carbs 8g

Ingredients:

For the grilled tofu skewers:

- 1 package of extra-firm tofu, drained and pressed for 30 minutes or longer
- 1/2 teaspoon of smoked paprika
- 2 tablespoons of water
- 1 tablespoon of honey
- 2 tablespoons of soy sauce
- 1/2 teaspoon of garlic powder

For the spicy peanut sauce:

- 1/4 cup of coconut milk
- 2 tablespoons of soy sauce
- 1/4 teaspoon of garlic powder
- 1/2 cup of creamy peanut butter
- 1 tablespoon of Sriracha
- 2 tablespoons of lime juice

Instructions:

- Squeeze the tofu block into eight sticks.
- Combine the tofu, soy sauce, smoked paprika, water, honey, and garlic powder inside a sealable plastic bag, seal, and toss to coat.
- Chill for at least 1 hour and up to 24 hours before grilling.
- Combine all of the spicy peanut sauce ingredients inside a small-sized mixing bowl; set aside or refrigerate till needed.

- Pour the marinade into a dish and set aside to use as a basting sauce before cooking.
- Thread the tofu onto metal skewers lengthwise.
- Preheat the griddle at medium-high heat.
- Spread a thin layer of olive oil on the griddle.
- Cook the skewers for 10 to 15 minutes, rotating occasionally, till char marks appear on both sides; baste frequently with the remaining marinade while they cook.
- Serve immediately with a dipping sauce of spicy peanut sauce.

7. Zucchini Almond and Gouda Meatballs

(Preparation time: 10 minutes | Cooking time: 30 minutes | Servings: 4 | Difficulty: Easy)

Per serving: Calories 280, Total fat 16g, Protein 24g, Carbs 15g

Ingredients:

- 2 eggs, beaten
- 1/2 cup of grated Gouda cheese
- 1 tablespoon of parsley, finely chopped
- 2 tablespoons of vegetable oil
- Salt and pepper to taste
- 1 cup of almond flour
- 3 zucchinis
- 1/2 cup of whole meal breadcrumbs

Instructions:

- Before cutting the zucchini into pieces, peel and wash it.
- Also, wash and finely slice the parsley.
- Then, in a skillet, heat the olive oil and cook the zucchini cubes with some water for about 15 minutes.
- After they're done, drain and mash finely inside a large-sized mixing bowl with a vegetable masher.
- Then, in a separate bowl, combine 5 tablespoons of almond flour and finely grated Gouda cheese.
- Inside a mixing bowl, combine the two eggs, oat flour, and parsley.
- Season using salt and pepper to taste.

- Set the zucchini filling aside, which should be the size of golf balls.
- Preheat your outdoor griddle at medium temperature.
- Spray the griddle top using cooking spray.
- Combine the oil and wholegrain breadcrumbs till the mixture is loose and crumbly.
- To make a croquette, roll each zucchini ball in the almond flour, then the eggs, and finally the breadcrumbs.
- Press the coating down to ensure that it adheres to the meatballs.
- Cook the meatballs on the griddle.
- Allow for 15 minutes or till golden brown.
- Serve immediately with your preferred sauce.

8. Peas and Cheddar Pie

(Preparation time: 10 minutes | Cooking time: 20 minutes | Servings: 4 | Difficulty: Easy)
Per serving: Calories 390, Total fat 5g, Protein 12g, Carbs 40g
Ingredients:

- 1 cup of peas
- 2 eggs
- Olive oil to taste
- 1 roll of short crust pastry
- Salt and pepper to taste
- 1/2 cup of cheddar cheese
- 2 red onions

Instructions:

- Before slicing onions, they should be peeled and washed.
- After rinsing the peas under running water, drain them.
- Heat a tablespoon of olive oil in a pan and sauté the onions for about 2 minutes.
- Cook for 5 minutes after adding the peas.
- Season using salt & black pepper before removing from the flame and setting aside to cool.
- Meanwhile, inside a mixing bowl, whisk the eggs with salt and black pepper.

- Combine the cheddar cheese cubes in a mixing bowl.
- Now add the onion and peas.
- After brushing the baking pan with olive oil, line it with shortcrust dough.
- Stuff the dough with the filling.
- Preheat the griddle at a high temperature.
- Place the baking pan on the griddle.
- Cook for approximately 20 minutes.
- After the quiche has finished cooking, remove it from the griddle and set it aside to cool for 10 minutes.
- After 10 minutes, slice it and arrange it on plates.

9. Eggplant and Ricotta Bundles

(Preparation time: 20 minutes | Cooking time: 25 minutes | Servings: 4 | Difficulty: Easy)

Per serving: Calories 350, Total fat 14g, Protein 16g, Carbs 30g

Ingredients:

- 1 egg
- 2 little eggplants
- Olive oil to taste
- 1 roll of vegan puff pastry
- ½ shallot
- 3 tablespoons of olive oil
- 1 cup of ricotta cheese
- Salt and Pepper to taste

Instructions:

- First, peel and wash the eggplants.
- After that, cut the eggplants into cubes.
- Boil them for about 20 minutes in salted water.
- Take them out of the water and thoroughly drain them.
- Meanwhile, cut the puff pastry into 8 squares.
- Also, cut the mozzarella into small pieces.

- Preheat the griddle at 370°F.
- Meanwhile, stuff each puff pastry square with a cube of eggplant and a dollop of ricotta.
- Create a bundle from each square.
- Whisk together 2 tablespoons of olive oil and egg.
- Now place the eggplant bundles on a baking sheet.
- Brush each bundle with the egg and olive oil.
- Cook for 35 to 40 minutes on the griddle, possibly extending the cooking time till the pastry is golden and crispy.
- Serve while the food is still hot.

10. Romaine Salad with Bacon & Blue Cheese

(Preparation time: 10 minutes | Cooking time: 15 minutes | Servings: 6 | Difficulty: Easy)

Per serving: Calories 283, Total fat 25g, Protein 13g, Carbs 6g

Ingredients:

- 12 pieces of thick-cut bacon
- 1/2 cup of blue cheese crumbles
- 3 romaine hearts

For the dressing:

- ¼ cup of light olive oil
- ¼ teaspoon of dried thyme
- ½ teaspoon of dried oregano
- ¼ teaspoon of dried parsley
- A little salt and black pepper
- ¼ teaspoon of Dijon mustard
- ¼ cup of balsamic vinegar

Instructions:

- Preheat one side of your griddle at medium-high and the other to high heat.
- On a medium-high griddle, cook the bacon for 5 to 8 minutes on each side.
- After slicing each romaine heart in half, set it aside.

- Brush a small amount of bacon oil across the flat side of each Romaine half with a brush.
- Place the romaine pieces, flat side down, on the grill's high heat temperature for about 30 seconds.
- Place the bacon on a plate lined using paper towels to cool before crumbling.
- On a separate platter, arrange the romaine halves.
- Whisk together the dressing ingredients inside a small-sized mixing bowl and drizzle over the romaine.
- To serve, top each romaine half with bacon and blue cheese crumbles.

11. Thyme Potato Focaccia

(Preparation time: 20 minutes | Cooking time: 20 minutes | Servings: 4 | Difficulty: Medium)

Per serving: Calories 350, Total fat 5g, Protein 6g, Carbs 39g

Ingredients:

- 1 cup of potatoes
- ½ cup of warm water
- 1 tablespoon of thyme needles
- Olive oil to taste
- 1 teaspoon of vegan brown sugar
- 1 1/4 cups of whole meal flour
- Salt and pepper to taste
- 1 teaspoon of brewer's yeast

Instructions:

- Begin with the potatoes, which should be thoroughly washed under running water without being peeled.
- Cook them for about 25 minutes inside a large-sized pot of boiling salted water.
- After they've been cooked, drain them and run them under cold water to peel them.
- Mash them using a potato masher and place them in a bowl.
- Inside a mixing bowl, combine the whole flour, baking powder, 2 tablespoons salt, sugar, and water.
- Knead the dough for at least 15 minutes, or till it is soft.

- Compress it using your hands and roll it into a ball. Allow for 2 hours of rising after covering with the cling film.

- Preheat your griddle at medium temperature.

- Cook for about 15 minutes with the pizza stone on top of the griddle.

- Place the dough in a round baking pan brushed using olive oil.

- Apply olive oil to the surface and roll it out using both hands.

- Season the baking pan with salt and thyme needles and place it on top of the pizza stone.

- Cook for approximately 20 minutes.

- If the focaccia is golden brown, remove it from the griddle; otherwise, heat for another 5 minutes.

- When it's done, remove it from the griddle and set it aside for 5 minutes to rest.

- After 5 minutes, cut it into 8 slices and serve.

12. Tofu and Ginger Stuffed Yellow Bell Peppers

(Preparation time: 10 minutes | Cooking time: 20 minutes | Servings: 4 | Difficulty: Easy)

Per serving: Calories 230, Total fat 8g, Protein 21g, Carbs 14g

Ingredients:

- 1 teaspoon of smoked paprika
- 4 yellow bell peppers
- 1 chopped red onion
- 1/2 cup of cubed tofu
- 1 tablespoon of freshly grated ginger
- Salt and pepper to taste
- 1 teaspoon of oregano

Instructions:

- Wash the bell pepper first to get rid of the pulp and seeds.
- In addition, wash and finely slice the red onion.
- Inside a large-sized mixing bowl, combine cubed tofu, salt, pepper, smoky paprika, red onion, freshly grated ginger, and oregano.
- Fill each pepper using a spoonful of the filling.

- Fill a baking dish halfway with peppers.
- Preheat your griddle at medium temperature.
- Cook the bell peppers on the griddle for about 20 minutes or till the red bell peppers are tender, and the tofu is golden.
- Serve while the food is still hot.

13. Soy Cheese and Bell Pepper Gazpacho

(Preparation time: 10 minutes | Cooking time: 15 minutes | Servings: 4 | Difficulty: Medium)

Per serving: Calories 130, Total fat 4g, Protein 13g, Carbs 10g

Ingredients:

- 6 tomatoes
- 1 teaspoon of apple cider vinegar
- ½ peeled & seedless cucumber
- 2 red bell peppers
- 1 small yellow pepper
- A stick of celery
- 4 drops of unsalted soy sauce
- 2 drops of Tabasco (or other hot sauce)
- Freshly ground pepper
- 1/2 cup of spreadable soy cheese
- 2 tablespoons of extra virgin olive oil
- Basil

Instructions:

- To begin, heat your griddle to the highest setting.
- Arrange the peppers and whole tomatoes in a pleasing pattern.
- Toast them on one side only on the griddle, being careful not to burn them: gazpacho contains raw vegetables, but the burnt part, which we will remove, will give the preparation a roasted scent.
- Remove the peppers and tomatoes' seeds, peels, and any blackened areas.

- Combine the tomatoes, peppers, celery, and peeled and seedless cucumber inside a mixing bowl with the vinegar and soy sauce; chill for around 20 minutes or till very cold.
- In a blender, blend the vegetables for a few seconds.
- Slowly incorporate the olive oil with a spoon till the desired consistency is reached.
- Refrigerate for at least 5/6 hours before serving, adding the Tabasco just before serving.
- Half an hour before serving, thinly slice a yellow pepper.
- In the meantime, make the soy cream cheese.
- Whisk the soy cheese lightly with a fork, adding a teaspoon of soymilk if necessary.
- To the soy cheese, add 4 finely chopped basil leaves and black pepper.
- In a pastry bag, chill the mixture till ready to use.
- Serve the gazpacho topped with a dollop of soy cream cheese.

14. Grilled Potato Chips with Lemon Mustard Sauce

(Preparation time: 15 minutes | Cooking time: 15 minutes | Servings: 4 | Difficulty: Medium)

Per serving: Calories 230, Total fat 9g, Protein 2g, Carbs 24g

Ingredients:

- 4 large potatoes
- 2 tablespoons of olive oil
- 1 teaspoon of salt

For the garlic mayonnaise:

- 2 cloves of garlic (minced)
- A pinch of salt
- 1/2 cup of mustard
- 1 tablespoon of lemon juice

Instructions:

- Preheat your griddle at medium temperature.
- Spray the griddle top using cooking spray.
- In the meantime, make potato chips.

- Using a mandolin slicer or a sharp knife, cut potatoes lengthwise into thin slices.
- Inside a large-sized mixing bowl, combine the potatoes with olive oil and salt.
- Arrange the potatoes on the griddle in a single layer.
- Cook for 5 to 8 minutes per side or till browned.
- Repeat with the rest of the potato slices.
- Meanwhile, make the lemon mustard.
- Garlic cloves should be peeled and minced before using.
- Combine mustard, garlic, lemon juice, and a pinch of salt inside a mixing bowl.
- Taste it to ensure that the flavor is to your liking. Make any necessary adjustments.
- Serve with grilled mustard-flavored potato chips.

15. Ratatouille

(Preparation time: 15 minutes | Cooking time: 25 minutes | Servings: 6 | Difficulty: Easy)

Per serving: Calories 189, Total fat 12g, Protein 3g, Carbs 15g

Ingredients:

- 2 pounds of eggplant, sliced into ¾-inch-thick rounds 1 pound of tomatoes, cored and halved
- 1 red onion, cut into ½-inch-thick slices & skewered
- ¼ cup of chopped fresh basil
- 3 tablespoons of sherry vinegar
- ¼ cup of extra-virgin olive oil, plus extra for brushing
- 1 tablespoon of minced fresh thyme
- 2 bell peppers, stemmed, seeded, & halved, each half cut into thirds
- 1 garlic clove, minced to paste
- 1½ pounds of zucchini or summer squash, sliced lengthwise into ½-inch-thick planks
- Salt and pepper, to taste

Instructions:

- Brush onion, bell peppers, eggplant, zucchini, and tomatoes with oil and sprinkle with salt and pepper. Combine 1/4 cup oil, vinegar, thyme, basil, and garlic in a large mixing bowl.

- Turn all of your griddle burners to high, cover, and heat the griddle for about 15 minutes. Turn up the heat on all of the burners to medium-high.

- Spray the griddle top using cooking spray.

- Cook, turning once, on the grill till the vegetables are soft and streaked with grill marks, about 10 to 12 minutes for onions, 8 to 10 minutes for eggplant and squash, 7 to 9 minutes for peppers, and 4 to 5 minutes for tomatoes. Take the vegetables out of the pan and set them aside to cool slightly.

- Cut the vegetables into 1/2-inch pieces and toss them in the oil mixture. Season using salt and black pepper and serve warm.

16. Glazed Tofu Steaks with Mango Salsa

(Preparation time: 10 minutes | Cooking time: 10 minutes | Servings: 6 | Difficulty: Medium)

Per serving: Calories 138, Total fat 9g, Protein 8g, Carbs 7g

Ingredients:

- 1 ¼ pound firm tofu, drained, cut lengthwise into four 1-inch thick "steaks."

- 1 bunch of fresh cilantro

- ¼ cup of lemon juice

- 1 teaspoon of blackstrap molasses

- 2/3 cup of white vegetable stock (below)

- 1 tablespoon of brown sugar

- 5 garlic cloves

- Black pepper, to taste

- 2 mangoes

- 1 small fresh pineapple

- ¼ cup of minced fresh ginger

- 1 tablespoon of crushed red pepper

Instructions:

- To make 1/2 cup cilantro, chop 1/2 cup and set aside 1 tablespoon for salsa.
- Inside a medium-sized baking dish, combine the cilantro, stock, lemon juice, garlic, red pepper, ginger, sugar, molasses, and black pepper. Toss in the tofu and combine thoroughly.
- Allow it to marinate at room temperature for 2 hours. Peel and finely chop the pineapple and mangoes, removing the skin and core of the pineapple and the pit of the mango.
- Combine the fruit and 1 tablespoon of the saved chopped cilantro in a medium-sized serving bowl. Allow the flavors to meld at room temperature.
- Preheat your griddle at medium heat. Drain the tofu and set aside the marinade.
- Spray the griddle top using cooking spray.
- Cook the tofu till lightly browned, around 4-5 minutes, sprinkling with the marinade frequently and rotating once. Serve the tofu steaks with the pineapple & mango mixture.

17. Balsamic-Glazed Veggie Kabobs

(Preparation time: 10 minutes | Cooking time: 10 minutes | Servings: 6 | Difficulty: Easy)

Per serving: Calories 298, Total fat 20g, Protein 6g, Carbs 28g

Ingredients:

- ½ cup of bell peppers, cubed into 1-inch chunks
- 1 teaspoon of garlic powder
- ½ cup of eggplant, cubed into 1-inch chunks
- 1 teaspoon of black pepper
- ½ cup of zucchini, cubed into 1-inch chunks
- 3 tablespoons of olive oil
- ½ cup of red onion, cubed into 1-inch chunks
- 1 teaspoon of sea salt
- 1/4 cup of balsamic glaze

Instructions:

- Preheat your griddle at medium-high.
- Alternately arrange vegetables on metal skewers.

- Place on a baking sheet or a piece of aluminum foil to catch the drips.
- Inside a small-sized mixing bowl, combine the salt, olive oil, garlic powder, and pepper; drizzle over skewers and turn to cover well.
- Apply a thin layer of olive oil to the griddle.
- Brush skewers using balsamic glaze and cook for 4 to 5 minutes on both sides till blackened, frequently basting till veggies are cooked.
- Serve the kabobs on a serving platter!

18. Gorgonzola and Potatoes Gratin

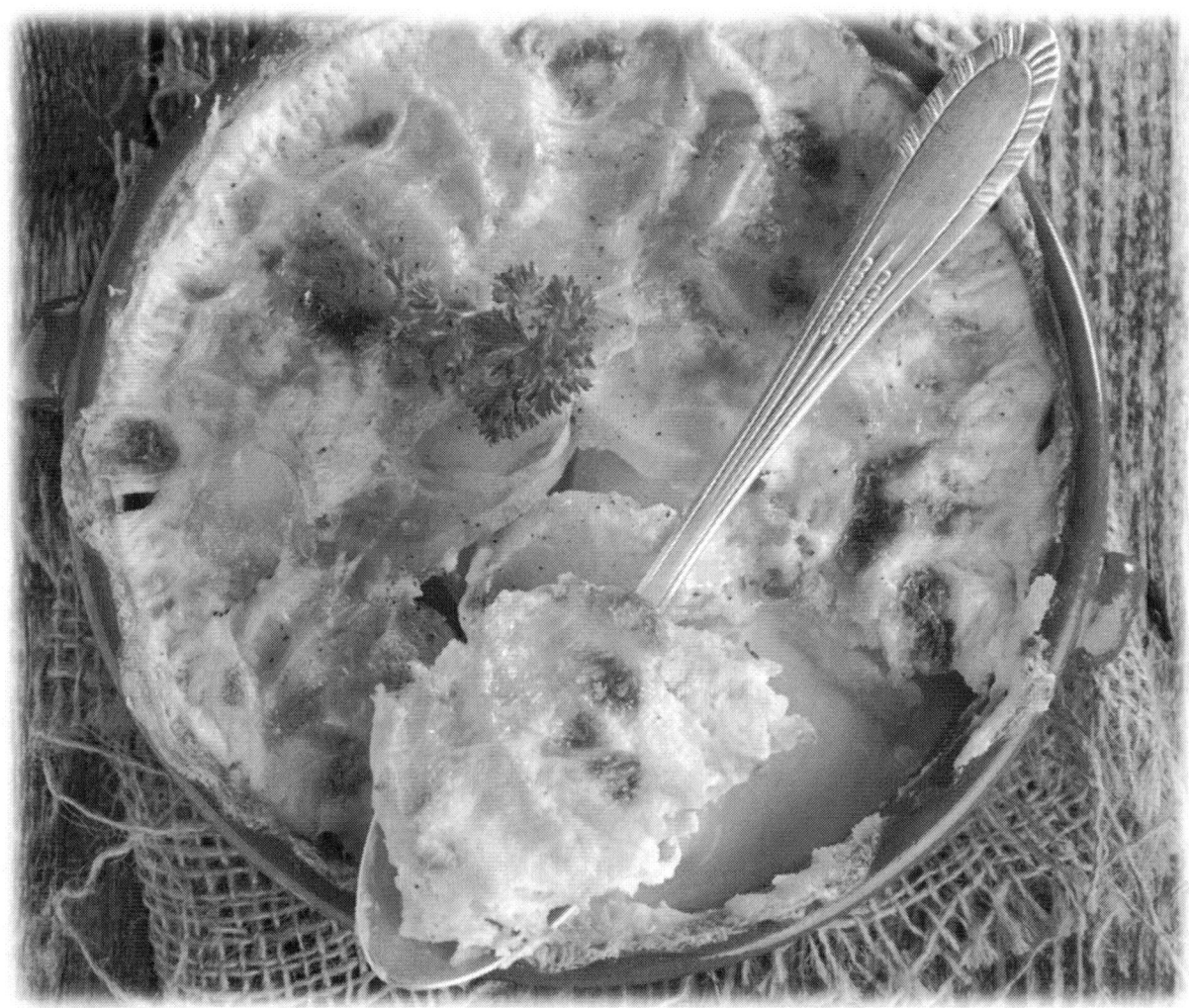

(Preparation time: 10 minutes | Cooking time: 40 minutes | Servings: 4 | Difficulty: Easy)
Per serving: Calories 420, Total fat 14g, Protein 15g, Carbs 38g

Ingredients:

- 6 medium potatoes, peeled
- 1/2 cup of Gorgonzola (cubed)
- 1 pinch of nutmeg
- ½ cup of soy milk
- 2 tablespoons of grated Parmesan cheese
- ½ cup of vegan béchamel
- 1 pinch of cinnamon

Instructions:

- Preheat the griddle at medium-high.
- Meanwhile, prepare the potatoes by washing, peeling, and thinly slicing them.
- Inside a mixing bowl, combine the soy milk, vegan béchamel, salt, pepper, cinnamon, and nutmeg.
- Gorgonzola should be cut into small cubes.
- Coat the potato slices in the milk mixture.
- Place the potato slices on a baking sheet and drizzle with the remaining béchamel mixture from the bowl.
- Place the baking pan on the griddle.
- Cook for about 15 minutes.
- After 5 minutes, sprinkle the Parmesan cheese evenly over the potatoes.
- Cook till the cheese melts and the gratin browns.
- While the gratin is still hot, serve it.

19. Smoked Cheesy Eggplant

(Preparation time: 15 minutes | Cooking time: 10 minutes | Servings: 4 | Difficulty: Easy)

Per serving: Calories 234, Total fat 14g, Protein 12g, Carbs 19g

Ingredients:

- 2 eggplants
- Olive oil
- 1 teaspoon of oregano

- Salt and pepper to taste

For the sauce:

- 1 cup of cooking cream
- 1/2 cup of cubed smoked cheese
- 1 pinch of smoked paprika
- Salt to taste

Instructions:

- First, prepare the eggplants.
- After peeling the eggplants, cut them into strips.
- Preheat the griddle at a high temperature.
- Spray the griddle top using cooking spray.
- Then add the eggplants and cook for about 3 to 5 minutes.
- Season using oregano, salt, and pepper to taste.
- Cook for another 7 minutes, stirring occasionally.
- Meanwhile, make the smoked cheese sauce. On the other side of your griddle place the saucepan.
- Allow the cooking cream to come to the boil before adding the smoked cheese cubes.
- Combine all of the ingredients and stir till the cheese is completely melted.
- Season using salt and paprika to taste.
- Make sure the eggplants are completely cooked. Season using salt and pepper to taste. Serve on a plate with the smoked cheese sauce.

20. Zucchini and Tomato Quiche

(Preparation time: 20 minutes | Cooking time: 20 minutes | Servings: 4 | Difficulty: Medium)

Per serving: Calories 270, Total fat 12g, Protein 16g, Carbs 24g

Ingredients:

- 4 tablespoons of smoked cheese
- Salt and black pepper to taste
- 12 cherry tomatoes
- Chives to taste

- 1 roll of short crust pastry
- Olive oil to taste
- 2 zucchinis

Instructions:
- Preheat the griddle at medium-temperature.
- Spray the griddle top using cooking spray.
- Before slicing the zucchini, it should be peeled and washed.
- Sauté the zucchini for about 5 minutes. Season using salt & pepper, mix well and remove from the griddle.
- Before slicing cherry tomatoes in half, they should be washed and dried.
- Cut the smoked cheese into cubes with a knife.
- Line a baking pan with puff pastry after brushing it using oil.
- Start with the zucchini, then the tomatoes, and finally the smoked cheese. Season using oil, salt, and pepper and sprinkle chives over the top.
- Preheat your griddle at a high temperature.
- Place the baking pan for 20 minutes with the lid closed.
- Once the baking pan has finished cooking, remove it from the griddle and set it aside to cool for 10 minutes.
- Slice the quiche into slices and arrange it on plates to serve.

21. Stuffed Yellow Bell Peppers

(Preparation time: 10 minutes | Cooking time: 20 minutes | Servings: 4 | Difficulty: Easy)

Per serving: Calories 230, Total fat 8g, Protein 21g, Carbs 14g

Ingredients:
- 4 yellow bell peppers
- 1 chopped red onion
- Salt and pepper to taste
- 1 tablespoon of freshly grated ginger
- 1 teaspoon of smoked paprika
- 1/2 cup of cubed tofu

- 1 teaspoon of oregano

Instructions:

- Wash the bell pepper first and discard the pulp and seeds.
- In addition, wash and finely slice the red onion.
- Inside a large-sized mixing bowl, combine cubed tofu, salt, pepper, smoky paprika, red onion, freshly grated ginger, and oregano.
- Fill each pepper with a spoonful of the filling.
- Fill a baking dish halfway with peppers.
- Preheat your griddle at medium temperature.
- Cook the bell peppers on the griddle for about 20 minutes or till the red bell peppers are tender, and the tofu is golden.
- Serve while the food is still hot.

22. Garlic, Bacon & Lemon Cauliflower Steaks

(Preparation time: 10 minutes | Cooking time: 15 minutes | Servings: 3 | Difficulty: Easy)

Per serving: Calories 210, Total fat 15g, Protein 8g, Carbs 17g

Ingredients:

- 2 large heads of cauliflower
- 2 lemons, zested & juiced
- 2 scallions, sliced thin, for garnish
- 1/4 teaspoon of red pepper flakes
- 2 slices of bacon or turkey bacon, chopped, for garnish
- 2 tablespoons of olive oil
- Sour cream, for garnish
- 2 cloves of garlic, finely minced
- Lemon wedges, for serving
- 2 teaspoons of sea salt, divided

Instructions:

- The outer leaves of each cauliflower head should be removed. Take out the stems.
- Trim the cauliflowers' sides using a large, sharp knife while still resting on their stems, then cut the remaining head into three thick "steaks" each.

- Combine the lemon zest, olive oil, lemon juice, garlic, sea salt, and red pepper inside a small-sized mixing bowl.
- Preheat your griddle at medium heat and coat it lightly using olive oil.
- Brush one side of each cauliflower steak using the lemon olive oil mixture and cook, seasoned side down, on a hot griddle.
- Brush the tops of the steaks with the olive oil mixture.
- Cook for 5-6 minutes or till the bottom begins to brown. Cook for another 5 minutes on the other side or till the cauliflower is soft.
- Take the steaks off the griddle. If desired, garnish with lemon wedges and sour cream, bacon, and chives.

23. Cauliflower and Spicy Cheddar Soufflé

(Preparation time: 10 minutes | Cooking time: 30 minutes | Servings: 4 | Difficulty: Medium)

Per serving: Calories 250, Total fat 15g, Protein 22g, Carbs 9g

Ingredients:

- 1 cup of cauliflower florets
- Olive oil
- 1 teaspoon of chopped jalapeno
- 1/4 cup of grated cheddar cheese
- 1 cup of vegan béchamel
- 4 eggs
- Salt and pepper to taste
- 1 teaspoon of chili powder

Instructions:

- To begin, cut the cauliflower into tiny florets.
- After that, the buds should be washed and dried.
- Cook the flowers in salted water for 10 minutes.
- Preheat your griddle at medium heat.
- Spray the griddle top using cooking spray.
- Sauté the cauliflower for around 4 to 5 minutes.

- Before transferring the cauliflower to a mixing glass, season with salt and pepper.
- Combine them till they form a thick, silky cream.
- In a mixing bowl, combine the cauliflower cream.
- Now is the time to separate the yolks and whites.
- In one bowl, combine the egg yolks and cauliflower; in another, combine the egg whites.
- Whisk till stiff peaks form in the egg whites.
- In a mixing bowl, combine the cauliflower and egg yolks with the béchamel sauce, jalapeno, grated cheddar cheese, chili powder, and a pinch of salt and pepper.
- Combine everything thoroughly.
- Gently fold in the egg whites to prevent them from dissolving.
- Fill oiled single-portion molds with the mixture to a third of their height.
- Preheat your griddle at medium heat.
- Place the soufflé on the griddle for about 25 minutes (at least).
- When they're done, remove them from the griddle and serve them immediately in the same baking dish.

24. Cumin Chili Potato Wedges

(Preparation time: 10 minutes | Cooking time: 20 minutes | Servings: 4 | Difficulty: Easy)

Per serving: Calories 343, Total fat 17g, Protein 5g, Carbs 42g

Ingredients:

- 3 large russet potatoes, scrubbed and cut into 1-inch-thick wedges
- 1 teaspoon of freshly ground black pepper
- 1 teaspoon of cumin
- 1/3 cup of olive oil
- 1 teaspoon of garlic powder
- 1 teaspoon of kosher salt
- 1 teaspoon of chili powder

Instructions:

- Set aside a small-sized bowl with the cumin, chili powder, salt, garlic powder, and pepper.
- Preheat the griddle at medium-high on one side and medium on the other.
- Spray the griddle top using cooking spray.

- Brush the potatoes using olive oil and cook till browned and crisp on both sides, about 2 to 3 minutes per side, on the hot side of the griddle.
- Transfer the potatoes to the cooler side of the grill, cover using foil, and cook for another 5 to 10 minutes or till cooked through.
- Remove the potatoes from the griddle and place them inside a large-sized mixing bowl. Toss the vegetables in the spice mixture to coat.
- Serve warm, and enjoy.

25. Parmesan-Garlic Asparagus

(Preparation time: 10 minutes | Cooking time: 10 minutes | Servings: 6 | Difficulty: Easy)

Per serving: Calories 108, Total fat 8g, Protein 6g, Carbs 4g

Ingredients:

- 3 tablespoons of parmesan cheese, shaved
- Sea salt, to taste
- 2 tablespoons of olive oil
- 1 pound of fresh asparagus
- 2 garlic cloves, minced
- Black pepper, to taste

Instructions:

- Preheat the griddle to medium-high heat. A thin layer of olive oil should be applied to the griddle.
- Remove the asparagus spears' bottoms.
- On a baking sheet, toss the asparagus with the olive oil and season using salt and pepper.
- Cook the asparagus in a row for 5 to 10 minutes or till char marks appear and they are tender when probed using a fork.
- On a baking sheet, toss the asparagus with the garlic and parmesan and serve warm.

Chapter 6: Appetizers, Snacks, and Desserts

1. Southwest Chicken Drumsticks

(Preparation time: 10 minutes | Cooking time: 30 minutes | Servings: 8 | Difficulty: Easy)

Per serving: Calories 165, Total fat 12g, Protein 10g, Carbs 2g

Ingredients:

- 2 tablespoons of taco seasoning
- 2 tablespoons of olive oil
- 2 lbs. of chicken legs

Instructions:

- Preheat your griddle at medium-high heat and coat it using a thin layer of oil.
- Brush the chicken legs with oil and season using taco seasoning.
- Cook the chicken legs for about 30 minutes on a hot griddle.
- Turn the chicken legs every 10 minutes.
- Serve.

2. Corn Cakes

(Preparation time: 10 minutes | Cooking time: 10 minutes | Servings: 10 | Difficulty: Easy)

Per serving: Calories 122, Total fat 4g, Protein 6g, Carbs 16g

Ingredients:

- 2 cups of corn
- 1/2 cup of cheddar cheese, shredded

- 1/2 cup of cornmeal
- 4 eggs
- 1/2 cup of flour
- 1 jalapeno, chopped
- 1/2 teaspoon of kosher salt
- 2/3 cup of green onions, sliced
- 1/2 teaspoon of pepper

Instructions:

- Inside a food processor, pulse the corn till it is coarsely chopped.
- Inside a mixing bowl, combine the corn and the remaining ingredients till well combined.
- Preheat the griddle at medium-high heat.
- Coat the griddle's surface using cooking spray.
- Form the mixture into patties and cook on a hot griddle till golden brown on both sides.
- Take pleasure in your meal.

3. Apple Cobbler

(Preparation time: 20 minutes | Cooking time: 55 minutes | Servings: 8 | Difficulty: Easy)

Per serving: Calories 152, Total fat 5g, Protein 2g, Carbs 26g

Ingredients:

- 8 Granny Smith apples
- 1 cup of sugar
- 1 stick of melted butter
- 2 cups of plain flour
- ½ cup of brown sugar
- 2 teaspoons of baking powder
- 1 ½ cup of sugar
- A pinch of salt
- 2 eggs

- 1 teaspoon of cinnamon

Instructions:

- Before placing apples in a bowl, they should be peeled and quartered. Combine the cinnamon and one cup of sugar in a mixing bowl. Set aside for one hour after thoroughly stirring to coat.
- Preheat your griddle at medium temperature.
- Inside a large-sized mixing bowl, combine the salt, baking powder, sugar, eggs, brown sugar, and flour. Crush till crumbs form.
- Arrange the apples on a baking dish. Drizzle the melted butter over the crumble topping.
- Cook for about 40 minutes on the griddle.

4. Caramel Bananas

(Preparation time: 15 minutes | Cooking time: 15 minutes | Servings: 4 | Difficulty: Easy)

Per serving: Calories 152, Total fat 2g, Protein 2g, Carbs 36g

Ingredients:

- 4 slightly green bananas
- ½ cup of sweetened condensed milk
- 2 tablespoons of corn syrup
- ½ cup of brown sugar
- 1/3 cup of chopped pecans
- ½ cup of butter

Instructions:

- Preheat your griddle at medium temperature.
- Inside a large-sized pot on the griddle, bring the milk, corn syrup, butter, and brown sugar to the boil. Simmer the mixture for 5 minutes. Constantly stir the mixture.
- Spray the griddle top using cooking spray.
- Cook the bananas on the griddle with the peels on for around 5 minutes. Cook for 5 minutes more on the other side. The peels will be black and easily split.
- To serve, place on a plate. Remove the banana ends and split the peel in half. Remove the banana skins and top with caramel. On top, sprinkle with pecans.

5. Smashed Cheddar Bacon Baby Potatoes

(Preparation time: 10 minutes | Cooking time: 30 minutes | Servings: 6 | Difficulty: Easy)

Per serving: Calories 429, Total fat 21g, Protein 16g, Carbs 36g

Ingredients:

- 2 pounds of baby potatoes
- 1 teaspoon of onion powder
- 1 pound of cooked crumbled bacon
- 1/3 cup of olive oil
- 1 small bunch of chopped spring onion
- 1 tablespoon of smoked paprika
- 2 cups of grated cheddar cheese
- 1 teaspoon of garlic powder
- 1/4 cup of sour cream
- 1 tablespoon of dried chives

Instructions:

- Cool baby potatoes at room temperature after microwaving or boiling them till fork tender.
- Inside a large-sized mixing bowl, combine the olive oil, garlic powder, onion powder, paprika, and chives. Toss the potatoes in the mixture to coat. Place the potatoes on a baking sheet lined using parchment paper or silicone. Flatten the potatoes with your palm or a spatula.
- Preheat your griddle at medium temperature.
- Spray the griddle top using cooking spray.
- Cook potatoes for around 20 to 30 minutes, rotating once, till brown and crispy. On top are cheddar, bacon, and onions. Cook for another 10 minutes or till the cheese is completely melted.
- Remove from the griddle and top with sour cream and additional green onions, if desired. Enjoy!

6. Crispy Kale Chips

(Preparation time: 15 minutes | Cooking time: 20 minutes | Servings: 4 | Difficulty: Easy)

Per serving: Calories 174, Total fat 8g, Protein 7g, Carbs 12g

Ingredients:

- 2 bunch of washed and stems removed kale leaves
- Sea salt to taste
- Extra virgin olive oil as needed

Instructions:

- Ensure the kale leaves are completely dry before placing them on a sheet tray. Season using salt and black pepper, then drizzle using olive oil.
- Preheat your griddle at medium temperature.
- With the sheet tray on the griddle, cook for about 20 minutes or till the kale is lightly browned and crispy. Enjoy!

7. Pumpkin Pie

(Preparation time: 10 minutes | Cooking time: 50 minutes | Servings: 6 | Difficulty: Easy)

Per serving: Calories 240, Total fat 12g, Protein 3g, Carbs 29g

Ingredients:

- 3 large eggs
- 1 frozen pie crust, thawed

- 15 ounces of pumpkin puree
- 1/3 cup of cream, whipping
- 1 teaspoon of pumpkin pie spice
- 4 ounces of cream cheese
- 1/2 cup of brown sugar

Instructions:

- Preheat your griddle at a medium temperature with the lid closed.
- Combine cream cheese, milk, puree, sugar, and spice inside a mixing bowl. Beat an egg into the mixture one at a time. Fill the pie crust halfway with the ingredients.
- Cook for around 50 minutes on the griddle or till the edges are brown and the pie is firm around the edges but slightly jiggly in the center. Allow to cool completely before adding the whipped cream. Serve and have a good time!

8. Chewy Peanut Butter Cookies

(Preparation time: 10 minutes | Cooking time: 25 minutes | Servings: 24 | Difficulty: Easy)

Per serving: Calories 240, Total fat 12g, Protein 5g, Carbs 27g

Ingredients:

- 1 cup of peanut butter
- 1 egg whole
- 1 cup of sugar

Instructions:

- Preheat your griddle at a medium-high temperature.
- Combine all of the ingredients inside a mixing bowl. Place dough portions on a baking sheet that has been greased and cook for around 15 to 20 minutes. Allow cookies to cool on the baking sheet for 5 minutes before eating!

9. Bacon Cheddar Slider

(Preparation time: 20 minutes | Cooking time: 15 minutes | Servings: 2 | Difficulty: Easy)

Per serving: Calories 160, Total fat 11g, Protein 10g, Carbs 12g

Ingredients:

- 6 bacon slices, cut in half
- 1/2 cup of sliced kosher dill pickles

- 1-pound of ground beef (80% lean)
- 1/2 teaspoon of garlic salt
- 6 (1 oz.,) sliced sharp cheddar cheese, cut in half
- 1/2 teaspoon of black pepper
- 1/2 teaspoon of onion
- 12 mini breads sliced horizontally
- 1/2 teaspoon of salt
- Sliced red onion
- 1/2 cup of mayonnaise
- Ketchup
- 2 teaspoons of creamy wasabi (optional)
- 1/2 teaspoon of garlic

Instructions:

- Combine the ground beef, onion powder, garlic salt, seasoned salt, garlic powder, and black pepper inside a medium-sized mixing bowl.
- Form the beef mixture into 12 equal portions and shape them into thin round patties (around 2 ounces each).
- Preheat your griddle at medium heat and coat it with a thin layer of oil.
- Cook the bacon on the griddle for about 5-8 minutes or till it is crispy. Place them aside.
- To make the sauce, combine the mayonnaise and horseradish inside a small bowl.
- Griddle them for 3-4 minutes on each side or till the internal temperature reaches 160°F.
- Place a slice of cheddar cheese on each burger while it is on the griddle or after it has been removed from the griddle.
- Spread a small amount of mayonnaise mixture, a piece of red onion, and a hamburger pate on the bottom half of each roll. Pickled slices, ketchup, and bacon.

10. Loaded Tater Tots

(Preparation time: 10 minutes | Cooking time: 50 minutes | Servings: 6 | Difficulty: Easy)
Per serving: Calories 333, Total fat 30g, Protein 6g, Carbs 14g

Ingredients:

- 1 can of rinsed and drained black beans
- 1 1/2 cups of leftover chili
- 1 cup of leftover queso
- 1/2 cup of cilantro chopped
- 2 pounds of frozen tater tots
- 1 sliced jalapeno
- 1/2 cup of sour cream
- 1 finely diced red onion

Instructions:

- Preheat your griddle at medium-high heat.
- Frozen tots should be spread out on a baking pan, and place the baking pan on the griddle.
- Cook for around 20 to 25 minutes or till the tots are crispy.
- Add a layer of warm chili, queso, and beans on top. Cook for an additional 15 minutes on the griddle.
- Remove from the griddle and serve with red onion, sour cream, cilantro, and jalapeno on top. Enjoy!

11. Brownie Bread Pudding

(Preparation time: 10 minutes | Cooking time: 30 minutes | Servings: 4 | Difficulty: Easy)

Per serving: Calories 300, Total fat 14g, Protein 4g, Carbs 44g

Ingredients:

- 1 teaspoon of baking soda
- 3 teaspoons of vanilla extract
- 1 pinch of salt
- 1/2 cup of bittersweet chocolate chips
- 4 cups of Leftover brownies, cut into 1" cubes
- 1 cup of heavy cream
- 4 eggs
- 1/4 cup of dried coconut flakes
- whipped cream
- 1/2 cup of sugar
- 2 cups of brown sugar
- 1/2 teaspoon of salt
- 2 sticks of butter
- 1/4 candied walnuts or pecans

Instructions:

- Preheat your griddle at medium heat and cover for 15 minutes.
- Inside a small-sized mixing bowl, combine heavy cream, eggs, sugar, vanilla, and salt. Mix everything thoroughly, and combine brownies and chips. Transfer to baking pan.
- Sprinkle coconut flakes on top after adding the mixture to a 9 x 13 baking pan that has been greased.
- Cook for around 45 minutes or till the edges are lightly browned and puffy, and the center is barely set.
- Melt the butter, salt, and sugar inside a medium-sized saucepan on the griddle.
- Cook till an instant-read thermometer registers 275°F. Remove the pan from the griddle and stir in the vanilla extract and baking soda. It is advised to proceed with caution because it may boil and steam.
- Top brownie bread pudding with candied walnuts and sweetened whipped cream. Enjoy!

12. Chocolate Chip Mint Cookies

(Preparation time: 10 minutes | Cooking time: 20 minutes | Servings: 24 | Difficulty: Easy)

Per serving: Calories 119, Total fat 6g, Protein 2g, Carbs 16g

Ingredients:

- 1/2 cup of melted butter
- 8 to 10 drops of food coloring
- 1/2 teaspoon of mint extract
- 1 package of chocolate chip cookie mixture

Instructions:

- With the lid closed, preheat your griddle at medium heat.
- Mix the mint essence and green food coloring into the chocolate cookie dough and bake according to the package directions. Combine all of the ingredients till completely smooth.
- Drop dough balls with a diameter of about 2 tablespoons onto a baking sheet lined using parchment paper.
- Cook for around 10 to 12 minutes on a griddle. Remove from the griddle and set aside for a few minutes to cool. Enjoy!

13. Tortilla Pizza

(Preparation time: 10 minutes | Cooking time: 10 minutes | Servings: 1 | Difficulty: Easy)

Per serving: Calories 336, Total fat 16g, Protein 26g, Carbs 15g

Ingredients:

- 1 tortilla

For the topping:

- 1/4 cup of tomatoes, chopped
- 2 teaspoons of onion, chopped
- 1/2 teaspoon of garlic, minced
- 1/4 teaspoon of dried oregano
- 3 tablespoons of mozzarella cheese, shredded
- 1/4 teaspoon of red chili flakes
- Salt & pepper to taste

Instructions:

- Combine tomatoes, onion, pepper, garlic, oregano, chili flakes, cheese, and salt to make a tortilla and spread the mixture on the tortilla.
- Preheat the griddle at medium-high heat.
- Coat the griddle's surface with cooking spray.
- Cover and heat on a hot griddle till the cheese melts.
- Take pleasure in your meal.

14. Loaded Nachos

(Preparation time: 15 minutes | Cooking time: 20 minutes | Servings: 4 | Difficulty: Easy)
Per serving: Calories 509, Total fat 34g, Protein 23g, Carbs 26g
Ingredients:

- 1/4 cup of sliced scallions
- 1 cup of cooked and shredded chicken breast
- 1/2 cup of fresh salsa
- 1 pound of cooked and cubed Tri-Tip
- 1/4 cup of sliced black olives
- 1 bag of tortilla chips
- 1/2 cup of guacamole
- 1 pound of cooked and sliced kielbasa sausage
- 1 1/2 cups of cheddar cheese
- 1 Small jar of jalapeños, sliced
- 1/2 cup of sour cream
- 1/4 cup of cilantro

Instructions:

- Preheat your griddle at medium heat.
- Distribute the tortilla chips evenly on a large dish. Add the sausage, chicken, olives, and tri-tip to the chips after the salsa.
- Scallions, jalapenos, and cheese are sprinkled on top of the nachos.
- Place the tray on the griddle for 10 to 15 minutes or till the cheese has melted and the nachos are fully cooked.

- On the side, there's guacamole, sour cream, and cilantro. Enjoy!

15. Apple Pear Crisp

(Preparation time: 10 minutes | Cooking time: 1-hour | Servings: 6 | Difficulty: Easy)

Per serving: Calories 340, Total fat 12g, Protein 5g, Carbs 42g

Ingredients:

- 5 pounds of diced apples and pears
- 1 1/4 cups of sugar
- 16 tablespoons of butter
- 1 cup of old fashioned oatmeal (not quick-cooking or instant)
- 1 1/2 cups of all-purpose flour
- 1 whole of lemon, juiced
- 3/4 cup of brown sugar
- 2 teaspoons of ground cinnamon
- 1/4 teaspoon of salt
- 1 whole of lemon zest
- 1/2 teaspoon of ground nutmeg

Instructions:

- A 9" x 13" baking dish should be sprayed using nonstick spray or brushed with butter.
- Inside a large-sized mixing bowl, whisk the butter using an electric stand mixer.
- On low, blend till the crumbs and butter are the size of peas. (Use your fingers or a hand-held dough blender if you don't have a dough blender.) Place them aside.
- Begin by combining the apples, lemon zest, and lemon juice inside a mixing bowl.
- Integrate the sugar, cinnamon, and nutmeg.
- Pour the fruit mixture into the pan. The filling should be used to cover the fruit.
- With the lid closed, preheat your griddle at medium heat.
- Bake for around 50-60 minutes, or till the fruit is tender and bubbling, and the top is golden.
- On top, serve with warm ice cream or whipped cream. Enjoy!

16. Soft Gingerbread Cookies

(Preparation time: 10 minutes | Cooking time: 15 minutes | Servings: 8 | Difficulty: Easy)

Per serving: Calories 120, Total fat 3g, Protein 3g, Carbs 19g

Ingredients:

- 1/4 cup of molasses
- 1/2 teaspoon of ground cinnamon
- 3/4 cup of butter, softened
- 1/2 teaspoon of baking soda
- 1/4 teaspoon of ground cloves
- 1 1/2 teaspoons of ground ginger
- 1 3/4 cups of all-purpose flour
- 1/2 cup of plus 4 tablespoons of granulated sugar
- 1 egg
- 1/3 cup of brown sugar
- 1/4 teaspoon of kosher salt

Instructions:

- Preheat your griddle at medium with a close lid.
- Set aside the flour, salt, cinnamon, baking soda, ginger, and cloves after mixing.
- Cream together brown sugar, 1/2 cup of granulated sugar, and butter on medium speed till soft and fluffy. Incorporate the egg and molasses, scraping down the bowl sides as you go.
- Stir in the dry mixture on low speed till well combined. Scrape again, then mix for 30 seconds.
- Roll the dough into tablespoon-sized balls, then roll them in the remaining four tablespoons of sugar to coat.
- Place the balls on a baking sheet lined using parchment paper two inches apart.
- Cook for about 10 minutes on the griddle or till lightly browned but still soft in the center.
- Enjoy!

17. Chili Con Queso

(Preparation time: 10 minutes | Cooking time: 1-hour | Servings: 8 | Difficulty: Easy)

Per serving: Calories 574, Total fat 39g, Protein 11g, Carbs 32g

Ingredients:

- 1 pound of Smoked gouda cheese
- 1 block of Velveeta cheese (2 lbs.)
- 1 pound of hot pork sausage
- 1/2 cup of cilantro chopped
- 4 tablespoons of Coffee rub
- 1 (10 oz.) of roasted diced tomatoes and green chilies
- 1 (10.5 oz.) cream of mushroom soup

Instructions:

- Preheat your griddle at medium heat.
- Cook the pig sausage on the griddle, breaking it up into small pieces as you go. Drain and discard the fat after removing the sausage.
- Place on the griddle a 4 to 5-quart cast-iron Dutch oven or another oven-safe dish. Chop the smoked Gouda into tiny 1-inch cubes and divide the Velveeta block into 5 to 6 large pieces. Combine all of the canned ingredients, including the liquid, in a mixing bowl.
- Finally, stir in the sausage and Coffee Rub.
- Cook the queso on the griddle for around 45 minutes, stirring every 4 to 5 minutes.
- The majority of the cilantro should be added during the last 5 minutes of cooking. Garnish with the remaining cilantro.
- Enjoy!

18. Stuffing Turkey Bacon Balls

(Preparation time: 15 minutes | Cooking time: 35 minutes | Servings: 8 | Difficulty: Easy)

Per serving: Calories 259, Total fat 11g, Protein 8g, Carbs 29g

Ingredients:

- 3 cups of prepared stuffing
- 1 can of cranberry sauce
- 6 slices of bacon

- 1 diced jalapeno
- 1 cup of cooked shredded turkey

Instructions:

- Preheat your griddle at medium and coat it using a thin layer of oil.
- Combine the cranberry sauce and jalapenos inside a small-sized saucepan. Bring to the boil on the griddle. Remove from the griddle and set aside to cool for about 4-5 minutes.
- To begin, place about 1/4 cup of stuffing in the palm of your hand. Make an indent with your thumb. Fill the indentation with a heaping spoonful of shredded turkey, then wrap the stuffing around the indentation to form a ball.
- Wrap half a slice of bacon around the stuffing ball and secure it with a toothpick if necessary. Continue till all of the bombs have been made.
- Place the stuffing balls on the griddle and cook for about 25-30 minutes, rotating once. Crispier bacon is preferable.
- Cranberry-jalapeno jelly on the side. Enjoy!

19. Caramel Pecan Brownie

(Preparation time: 15 minutes | Cooking time: 50 minutes | Servings: 6 | Difficulty: Easy)

Per serving: Calories 250, Total fat 13g, Protein 3g, Carbs 30g

Ingredients:

- 1 cup of all-purpose flour
- 1/4 cup of butter
- 3/4 cup of Pecans, halves
- 1.8 cups of brown sugar
- 3/4 cup of heavy cream
- 1/2 cup of cocoa powder
- 6 tablespoons of butter, melted
- 3 large eggs
- 1/2 teaspoon of salt
- 3/4 teaspoon of baking soda
- 6 ounces of chocolate, chopped

Instructions:

- With the lid closed, preheat your griddle at medium heat.

- To make the Pecan-Caramel Sauce, roast pecans in a 9-inch cast-iron pan over the griddle. After 5 minutes, stir to make sure everything is well combined. 1/4 cup of butter and 1/2 cup of brown sugar should be combined.

- Carefully place 1/2 cup of heavy cream on top of the pecans. Return the pan to the griddle and whisk in the cream. Take them off the griddle.

- Inside a mixing bowl, combine brown sugar, flour, baking soda, cocoa powder, and salt. Melted butter, egg, and cream should be combined.

- Cut milk should be folded in. Make a ring of brownie batter around it.

- Cook for around 35-40 minutes on the griddle or till a toothpick inserted into the center comes out clean.

- Remove from the griddle and set aside for 10 minutes to cool. Served with a scoop of vanilla ice cream. Enjoy!

20. Cherry Cobbler

(Preparation time: 10 minutes | Cooking time: 30 minutes | Servings: 8 | Difficulty: Easy)

Per serving: Calories 292, Total fat 5g, Protein 3g, Carbs 50g

Ingredients:

- 5 cups of fresh or frozen whole cherries, pitted
- 1 1/2 cups of all-purpose flour
- 2 cups of sugar
- 1 1/2 teaspoons of baking powder
- 8 tablespoons of cold unsalted butter
- 3/4 teaspoon of salt
- 1 orange zest
- 1/2 cup of sour cream
- 3 tablespoons of cornstarch
- lemon juice
- 1 lemon zest
- whipped cream
- 1/2 teaspoon of vanilla extract

- turbinado sugar

Instructions:

- To make the topping, combine flour, sugar, baking powder, and salt. Blend in the peas and broken crackers with the chilled butter.
- Fold in the sour cream till everything is well combined.
- Combine sugar, cornstarch, and salt to make the filling. In a separate bowl, combine the cherries, lemon juice, orange zest, and vanilla.
- Half-fill a baking dish with cherry filling, then top with cobbler topping.
- Preheat your griddle at medium heat, lid closed.
- Cook for around 35-45 minutes or till the cobbler's top is lightly browned and bubbling. It had thickened to a syrup consistency.
- Add whipped cream on top. Enjoy!

21. Sausage Mini Rolls

(Preparation time: 15 minutes | Cooking time: 30 minutes | Servings: 4 | Difficulty: Medium)

Per serving: Calories 319, Total fat 27g, Protein 6g, Carbs 13g

Ingredients:

- 2 pounds of uncooked sausage
- 3/4 cup of dry mustard
- 1 small diced onion
- 4 beaten egg yolks
- 1/2 cup of honey
- Ground sage
- 17 1/2 ounces of puff pastry frozen
- 3/4 cup of white vinegar distilled

Instructions:

- Inside a small-sized mixing bowl, combine the mustard and vinegar to make the mustard. Wrap in plastic wrap and set aside at room temperature overnight to allow the flavors to develop. Combine the honey, egg yolks, and mustard mixture inside a small-sized heavy pot. Cook, stirring frequently, for 7 minutes or till the sauce has thickened. Allow to cool before storing in the fridge till ready to use.
- Toss the sausage and onion inside a medium-sized mixing bowl till well combined. Roll out each thawed sheet of puff pastry (there should be two per box) into an 11 by 10-1/2-inch rectangle on a lightly floured work surface.
- Cut each rectangle into three 3-1/2-inch-wide strips with a pizza cutter or knife. Place one of the puff pastry strips in the center. Wet your hands and shape a piece of sausage into a tube shape.
- Wrap the dough around the sausage and seal the seams with an egg. Place all of the rolls on the work surface, seam side down, and lightly brush the tops with the egg.
- Rep with the remaining sausage and puff pastry. Cut the rolls into 1-1/2-inch pieces and place them on a parchment-lined rimmed baking sheet. Allow about an inch between rolls.
- Preheat your griddle at medium heat.
- Spray the griddle top using cooking spray.
- Cook for about 25 minutes, or till the dough is golden brown, and the meat is thoroughly cooked. Serve with honey mustard on the side.

22. Southwestern-Style Stuffed Peppers

(Preparation time: 15 minutes | Cooking time: 40 minutes | Servings: 6 | Difficulty: Easy)

Per serving: Calories 638, Total fat 33g, Protein 48g, Carbs 35g

Ingredients:

- 6 large-sized red bell peppers
- 1 diced small onion
- 2 cups of cooked white rice
- 1 cup of corn
- 2/3 cup of salsa
- 2 tablespoons of Cajun seasoning
- 1 cup of rinsed and drained black beans
- 2 cloves of minced garlic
- 1 1/2 cups of grated Monterey jack cheese

For the stuffing:

- 1 pound of ground beef

Instructions:

- Underneath cold running water, thoroughly rinse each pepper.
- Using a paring knife, cut the ribs and seeds in half lengthwise through the stem.
- Preheat your griddle at a medium temperature and coat it using a thin layer of oil.
- Brown the ground beef on the griddle, breaking it up using a wooden spoon to make the stuffing.
- Add the onions and garlic. Time to cook: 2-3 minutes. Combine the Cajun seasoning, black beans, salsa, rice, and corn. Cook for another 5 minutes or till the flavors have combined. Fill each half pepper halfway with the filling.
- Arrange the peppers on the griddle, stuffing side up, between the rungs. Cook for approximately 40 minutes.
- Evenly distribute the grated cheese over the peppers. Cook for 5 minutes more or till the cheese is completely melted.
- Enjoy!

23. Caramelized Bourbon Pears

(Preparation time: 10 minutes | Cooking time: 30 minutes | Servings: 4 | Difficulty: Easy)

Per serving: Calories 135, Total fat 6g, Protein 10g, Carbs 22g

Ingredients:

- 2 tablespoons of butter, melted
- 1/4 cup of brown sugar
- 3 whole slices of ripe pears,
- 1 teaspoon of vanilla extract
- 1/2 teaspoon of salt
- 1/4 cup of bourbon

Instructions:

- With the lid closed, preheat your griddle at medium.
- Pears must be peeled and cored before cooking. Place them inside a baking dish that has been sprayed with butter.
- Combine the brown sugar, butter, bourbon, vanilla, cinnamon, and salt inside a small-sized mixing bowl. Pour over the pears the bourbon mixture.
- Place the baking dish on the griddle, cover, and cook for around 30-35 minutes or till the pears are tender.
- On a serving plate, drizzle the caramelized bourbon mixture over the pears.
- Serve warm with vanilla ice cream. Enjoy!

24. Irish Coffee Pie

(Preparation time: 20 minutes | Cooking time: 45 minutes | Servings: 6 | Difficulty: Medium)

Per serving: Calories 104, Total fat 5g, Protein 2g, Carbs 7g

Ingredients:

- 3 tablespoons of Coffee, instant
- 16 Ritz Crackers
- 4 tablespoons of unsalted butter
- 1/2 cup of sugar
- 4 tablespoons of Lindt Excellence 70% Cocoa Bar
- 12 cookies of Oreo
- 5 yolk of an egg
- 1 1/2 cups of heavy cream

- 2 tablespoons of Bailey's Irish Cream

Instructions:

- With the lid closed, preheat your griddle at medium heat.
- To make the crust, pulse ritz, Oreos, and melted butter inside a food processor. Press the mixture into an 8" pie plate using your hands or the base of a cup.
- Bring heavy cream to boil inside a medium-sized saucepan on the griddle. Combine the sugar, Bailey's Irish Cream, and instant coffee. Whisk the sugar till it is completely dissolved.
- Place a deep baking dish filled with pie filling on the griddle.
- Cook for approximately 10 minutes. Set aside after removing from the griddle.
- Preheat your griddle at medium temperature.
- Melt chocolate inside a metal mixing bowl over a double boiler.
- Whisk the egg yolks in a separate bowl before adding the cream mixture. Incorporate the chocolate gradually. So that the yolks do not curdle, the cream and chocolate should be barely warmed.
- Using the filling, fill the pie crust. Cook for 30-35 minutes at medium heat or till the center is just set. Allow to cool completely on a wire rack. Whipped cream on top. Enjoy!

25. Asparagus Wrapped in Bacon

(Preparation time: 10 minutes | Cooking time: 30 minutes | Servings: 6 | Difficulty: Easy)

Per serving: Calories 71, Total fat 3g, Protein 6g, Carbs 1g

Ingredients:

- 15 - 20 spears of fresh asparagus (around 1 pound)
- Olive oil (extra virgin)
- 5 slices of bacon, thinly sliced
- 1 teaspoon of salt & pepper

Instructions:

- Trim the ends of the asparagus and trim them all to the same length.
- Make three bundles out of the asparagus spears. Then, spray them using olive oil.
- Wrap a piece of bacon around each bundle. When done, season the wrapped bundle with salt and black pepper or your favorite rub.
- Preheat your griddle at medium heat.
- Spray the griddle top using cooking spray.

- Griddle the wraps for 25 to 30 minutes, depending on their thickness. The asparagus should be nice and soft, and the bacon should be crispy.

26. Parmesan-Herb Popcorn

(Preparation time: 15 minutes | Cooking time: 25 minutes | Servings: 2 | Difficulty: Easy)

Per serving: Calories 227, Total fat 18g, Protein 7g, Carbs 11g

Ingredients:

- 4 tablespoons of butter
- 2 teaspoons of Italian seasoning
- 1 teaspoon of garlic powder
- 1/2 cup of grated parmesan cheese
- 1 teaspoon of salt
- 1/4 cup of popcorn kernels

Instructions:

- Preheat your griddle at a medium temperature.
- Melt the butter inside a small-sized saucepan on the griddle.
- Combine the garlic powder, Italian seasoning, and salt. Place the pan on the counter after removing it from the griddle.
- In a brown paper bag, place 1/4 cup of popcorn. To seal the bag, fold the top twice. Microwave the bag on high for 1 to 2 minutes or till each pop lasts about 5 seconds.
- Carefully open the container and empty the contents into a large mixing bowl.
- Toss the popcorn with the butter mixture in a mixing bowl.
- Popcorn should be cooked on the griddle in a baking pan.
- Remove from the griddle after about 10 minutes of cooking.
- Before serving, toss with parmesan cheese. Enjoy!

27. Lemon Bars

(Preparation time: 20 minutes | Cooking time: 1-hour | Servings: 8 | Difficulty: Medium)

Per serving: Calories 180, Total fat 8g, Protein 2g, Carbs 24g

Ingredients:

- 10 tablespoons of unsalted butter, cub
- 2 eggs
- 1 1/2 cups of sugar
- 3 egg yolk
- 1 1/2 teaspoons of cornstarch
- 4 tablespoons of unsalted butter
- sea salt
- 1/4 cup of granulated sugar
- 1 tablespoon of lemon zest
- 1/4 cup of olive oil
- 1 1/4 cups of flour
- 3/4 cup of lemon juice
- 3 tablespoons of powdered sugar
- 1/4 teaspoon of fine sea salt

Instructions:

- With the lid closed, preheat your griddle at medium temperature.
- Inside a mixing bowl, combine the lemon juice, sugar, eggs, yolks, cornstarch, and fine sea salt. Place a baking sheet or a cake pan on the griddle. Cook for about 30 minutes, whisking halfway.
- Set aside after removing from the griddle.
- Half-fill a pot with water. Bring the griddle to the boil. Bring the water to the boil for about 60 seconds. Remove from the griddle and place on a plate. Combine the chilled butter and lemon zest in a mixing bowl.
- Combine the granulated sugar, flour, confectioners' sugar, lemon zest, and salt inside a food processor. Add the butter and pulse till a crumbly dough forms. Press the dough into a 9" 9" baking dish using parchment paper hanging over two edges.
- Preheat your griddle at medium temperature.
- Cook for around 30-35 minutes or till the crust is lightly browned.
- Remove the pan from the griddle and top with the lemon filling.
- Return the pan to the griddle for another 15-20 minutes or till the filling is just set.

- Allow to completely cool before cutting into bars, just before serving, dust with icing sugar and flaky sea salt. Enjoy!

28. Blueberry Buckle Coffee Cake

(Preparation time: 20 minutes | Cooking time: 50 minutes | Servings: 10 | Difficulty: Medium)

Per serving: Calories 160, Total fat 4g, Protein 3g, Carbs 30g

Ingredients:

For the blueberry buckle:

- 2 cups of all-purpose flour
- 3/4 cup of granulated sugar
- 1 large egg
- 1 teaspoon of lemon zest
- 8 Tablespoon of butter, softened
- 1/2 teaspoon of salt
- 2 teaspoons of cinnamon
- 1 Tablespoon of lemon juice
- 1/2 cup of milk
- 2 1/2 Teaspoon of baking powder
- 1 teaspoon of vanilla extract
- 2 cups of fresh blueberries

For the topping:

- 8 tablespoons of butter
- 1 1/4 cups of all-purpose flour
- 1/4 teaspoon of salt
- 3/4 cup brown sugar
- 1/2 Teaspoon of cinnamon

Instructions:

- With the lid closed, preheat your griddle at a medium temperature.
- Cream the butter and sugar for about 5 minutes in an electric blender using the paddle attachment. Include the egg completely.

- Add 1 teaspoon of lemon juice and vanilla extract. Thoroughly combine.
- Combine the flour, salt, cinnamon, and baking powder. First, add half of the flour mixture, followed by half of the milk.
- Alternately add the flour and milk till the batter is completely combined.
- Fill an 8x8 baking sheet halfway with the mixture and evenly distribute it with a spatula. Blueberries were sprinkled on top.
- Combine the sugar, flour, salt, and cinnamon.
- Mix in the butter till the mixture is crumbly.
- Sprinkle streusel on top of the blueberries.
- Cook the blueberry buckle on the griddle for around 45 to 50 minutes or till done and lightly browned. Allow cooling for a few minutes before serving. This dish is delicious either warm or cold.

29. Atomic Buffalo Turds

(Preparation time: 15 minutes | Cooking time: 1 hour 30 minutes | Servings: 10 | Difficulty: Medium)

Per serving: Calories 198, Total fat 17g, Protein 8g, Carbs 3g

Ingredients:

- 10 bacon strips, thinly sliced & halved
- 1 teaspoon of smoked paprika
- ½ teaspoon of red pepper flakes
- 10 jalapeno peppers
- ¾ cup of cheddar cheese blend & shredded Monterey Jack
- 1 cup of regular cream cheese (at room temp)
- Little Smokies sausages
- 1 teaspoon of garlic powder

Instructions:

- After washing the jalapenos, cut them in half lengthwise. Remove all of the seeds and veins using a spoon or a paring knife, as desired.
- Set aside the jalapenos that you scooped out on a griddle pan.
- Inside a small-sized mixing bowl, combine the shredded cheese, garlic powder, cream cheese, paprika, cayenne pepper, and red pepper flakes. They must be thoroughly combined.

- Gather your hollowed-out jalapenos and stuff them with the cream cheese mixture.
- Fill each of the cheese-stuffed jalapenos with your Smokies sausage.
- Wrap each loaded jalapeno and its sausage in thinly sliced and halved bacon strips.
- Bring some toothpicks with you. Use these to keep the bacon securely attached to the sausage.
- Preheat your griddle at medium heat.
- Spray the griddle top using cooking spray.
- Cook your jalapeno peppers on the griddle for about 90 to 120 minutes at medium heat. Cook the bacon till it is nice and crispy.
- Set the atomic buffalo turds aside for 5 minutes to cool.
- Serve!

30. Loaded Potatoes

(Preparation time: 15 minutes | Cooking time: 1 hour 35 minutes | Servings: 4 | Difficulty: Easy)

Per serving: Calories 338, Total fat 16g, Protein 10g, Carbs 35g

Ingredients:

- 6 Yukon gold potatoes
- 1/2 cup of melted butter
- 1 bunch of thinly sliced green onions
- Salt & black pepper
- 1 cup of sour cream
- 8 slices of bacon
- 1 1/2 cups of grated cheddar cheese, divided

Instructions:

- Preheat your griddle at a medium and coat it using a thin layer of oil.

- Pierce the potatoes using a fork before placing them directly on the griddle. Cooking time is approximately 1 hour.

- Cook bacon for about 20 minutes on the griddle; remove, cool, and crumble.

- Remove the potatoes from the griddle and set aside to cool for about 15 minutes.

- Cut each potato in half lengthwise to make long halves. To make a boat, scrape out about 70% of the potato with a small spoon, leaving a thick layer of potatoes near the skin.

- Put any leftover potatoes in a dish and set aside. Mash the remaining potato lightly with a fork; stir in the sour cream, butter, and 1/2 cup of the cheese; season using salt and black pepper.

- Fill the potato skins using the potato mixture, then top with additional bacon and cheese.

- Return to the griddle for another 10 minutes or till thoroughly warmed and the cheese has melted as a garnish; top with additional sour cream and green onions. Enjoy!

Chapter 7: Fish and Seafood Recipes

1. Roasted Sheet Pan Salmon with Spring Vegetables and Pesto

(Preparation time: 15 minutes | Cooking time: 20 minutes | Servings: 6 | Difficulty: Easy)

Per serving: Calories 490, Total fat 28g, Protein 29g, Carbs 21g

Ingredients:

- 1 bunch of asparagus, trimmed
- 3 tablespoons of olive oil, divided
- Kosher salt & freshly ground black pepper
- 1 lemon, zested
- 6 (4 oz. each) of salmon, skin-on, pin bones removed
- Fresh basil leaves, for garnish
- 2 lemons, halved
- 1 1/2 cups of cherry tomatoes, rinsed & halved

- 1 pound of sugar snap peas, ends trimmed
- 1/2 cup of fresh pesto

Instructions:

- Preheat your griddle at medium heat. Line a large baking sheet or roasting pan using parchment paper.
- After cleaning the fish, rinse it and pat it dry with a paper towel.
- Brush the salmon on all sides with 2 tablespoons olive oil, then season generously with salt and black pepper. Place the salmon on a sheet tray, skin side up (or down if you prefer), with two inches gap between each piece.
- Inside a mixing bowl, combine the snap peas, asparagus, and cherry tomatoes. Combine the vegetables, the remaining tablespoon of olive oil, 1/2 teaspoon of salt, and a fresh grind of pepper. Arrange the vegetables on the sheet pan in an even layer.
- Place the sheet pan on top of the griddle. Also, chop the lemons and place them cut-side down on the griddle near the front for about 5 minutes.
- Remove the lemons from the griddle after 5 minutes and combine them with the vegetables. Cook for another 5 minutes, or till the fish reaches an internal temperature of 140°F and flakes easily with a fork.
- After removing the sheet pan from the griddle, set it aside. Drizzle the pesto over the fish and vegetables on a serving plate. Squeeze the grilled lemon over the fish and vegetables before serving. Toss the fish with the lemon zest and a few basil leaves to garnish. Serve right away. Enjoy!

2. Spicy Asian BBQ Shrimp

(Preparation time: 15 minutes | Cooking time: 25 minutes | Servings: 4 | Difficulty: Easy)

Per serving: Calories 197, Total fat 7g, Protein 24g, Carbs 6g

Ingredients:

- 2 tablespoons of minced ginger
- 6 cloves of minced garlic
- 1 minced jalapeño
- 1 stalk of minced green onions
- 1/4 cup of brown sugar
- 2 tablespoons of tomato paste
- 1 teaspoon of kosher salt
- 3 teaspoons of canola oil

- 1/2 cup of diced onion
- 1 tablespoon of rice vinegar
- 1/3 cup of soy sauce
- 1 teaspoon of minced jalapeño
- 2 teaspoons of grated ginger
- 1 pound of jumbo shrimp, peeled & deveined
- 1/2 teaspoon of sesame oil

Instructions:

- Combine the shrimp, green onion, oil, garlic, ginger, jalapeno, and salt inside a large mixing bowl. To coat the shrimp, thoroughly whisk together all of the ingredients. While you're making the sauce, marinate the shrimp.
- Preheat your griddle at medium heat.
- Heat the canola oil inside a saucepan on the griddle for the sauce. Sauté the garlic, jalapeno, ginger, and onion for about 3 minutes. Bring them to the boil, along with the soy sauce and brown sugar.
- Cook for 8 minutes on the griddle, covered, or till the onion is tender. Allow for a brief period of cooling before transferring it to a blender. Blend in the remaining sauce ingredients till the purée is smooth.
- Apply a thin layer of oil to the griddle's surface.
- Using metal skewers, skewer the shrimp. On the griddle, cook the shrimp skewers for 3 to 5 minutes on each side or till pink and opaque.
- Brush the shrimp skewers with the sauce you've made after removing them from the griddle. Enjoy!

3. Lobster Tails with Citrus Butter

(Preparation time: 10 minutes | Cooking time: 40 minutes | Servings: 4 | Difficulty: Easy)

Per serving: Calories 210, Total fat 20g, Protein 21g, Carbs 9g

Ingredients:

- 2 minced garlic cloves
- 4 lobster tails
- Salt & freshly ground black pepper, to taste
- ½ cup of butter, melted
- 2 teaspoons of fresh lemon juice

Instructions:

- Preheat your griddle at medium heat.
- Combine all ingredients, except the lobster tails, in a metal pan and stir well.
- Cook for about 10 minutes on the griddle with the pan.
- In the meantime, remove the top of the lobster shell to expose the meat.
- Remove the butter mixture from the griddle and set aside.
- Apply a thin layer of oil to the griddle's surface.
- Coat the lobster meat in the melted butter.
- Cook the lobster tails on the griddle for about 15 minutes, basting halfway through with the butter mixture.
- Remove from the griddle and serve immediately.

4. Scallops with Lemony Salsa Verde

(Preparation time: 10 minutes | Cooking time: 10 minutes | Servings: 2 | Difficulty: Easy)

Per serving: Calories 267, Total fat 10g, Protein 32g, Carbs 14g

Ingredients:

- 1 tablespoon of olive oil, plus more for grilling
- Sea salt for seasoning
- 12 large sea scallops, side muscle removed

For the Lemony Salsa Verde:

- ½ cup of finely chopped fresh cilantro
- 1 small shallot, finely chopped
- ¼ cup of chopped fresh chives
- ½ lemon, with peel, seeded & chopped
- ¼ teaspoon of sea salt
- 5 tomatillos, peeled & pulsed in a blender
- ¼ teaspoon of black pepper
- 1 garlic clove, finely chopped
- ¾ cup of finely chopped fresh parsley
- ¼ cup of olive oil

Instructions:

- Inside a small-sized mixing bowl, combine the ingredients for the Lemony Salsa.
- Preheat the griddle at medium-high heat after brushing it with olive oil.
- Toss scallops in 1 tablespoon olive oil and season using salt.
- Cook the scallops for 45 seconds to 1 minute on the griddle, rotating once. Cook for an additional minute before removing from the griddle.
- Top the scallops with a lemony salsa verde.

5. Tuna Meatloaf with Lemon and Capers

(Preparation time: 10 minutes | Cooking time: 30 minutes | Servings: 4 | Difficulty: Medium)

Per serving: Calories 303, Total fat 14g, Protein 30g, Carbs 17g

Ingredients:

- 17.6 oz. of tuna in oil
- Salt & pepper to taste
- 4 tablespoons of grated Parmesan cheese
- 2 tablespoons of capers
- 3 eggs
- Olive oil to taste
- 4 tablespoons of breadcrumbs
- 1 lemon

Instructions:

- After rinsing the capers, squeeze them. Place them on a cutting board and chop them finely.
- Inside a mixing bowl, drain the tuna and mash it with a fork.
- After the lemon has been washed and dried, grate the zest.
- Inside a mixing bowl, combine the eggs, breadcrumbs, salt, capers, parmesan, lemon zest, and pepper.
- Mix with a fork till the mixture is uniform and dense.
- A large piece of aluminum foil should be sprayed with olive oil.
- Place the meatloaf ingredients inside and roll them up to form a meatloaf.

- Preheat your griddle at medium heat.
- Spray the griddle top using cooking spray.
- Cook the meatloaf on the griddle for about 30 minutes.
- Remove the meatloaf from the griddle after 10 minutes of turning and set aside for 10 minutes.
- After 10 minutes, remove the aluminum foil and slice the meatloaf.
- Place the meatloaf on serving platters and serve.

6. Spiced Snapper with Mango and Red Onion Salad

(Preparation time: 10 minutes | Cooking time: 20 minutes | Servings: 4 | Difficulty: Medium)

Per serving: Calories 211, Total fat 6g, Protein 24g, Carbs 18g

Ingredients:

- Olive oil, plus more for griddle
- 2 red snappers, cleaned
- Extra-virgin olive oil for drizzling
- Sea salt
- ⅓ cup of tandoori spice
- Lime wedges, for serving

For the salsa:

- 1 bunch of cilantro, coarsely chopped
- 3 tablespoons of fresh lime juice
- 1 small red onion, thinly sliced
- 1 ripe but firm mango, peeled and chopped

Instructions:

- Combine the mango, lime juice, onion, cilantro, and a generous pinch of salt inside a medium-sized mixing bowl; drizzle with olive oil and toss to coat.
- On a chopping board, dry the snapper with paper towels. Slash crosswise on a diagonal all along the body on both sides, cutting all the way down to the bones using a sharp knife.
- Season the fish both inside and out with salt. Coat the fish in tandoori spice.
- Preheat your griddle at medium-high heat after brushing it using oil.
- Cook for 10 minutes, turning once or twice, or till the skin is puffy and browned.
- Cook for another 8 to 12 minutes or till the other side is lightly browned and the skin is puffy.
- Place on a serving platter.
- Top with lime wedges and mango salad.

7. Cedar-Plank Salmon with Mango Salsa

(Preparation time: 10 minutes | Cooking time: 30 minutes | Servings: 4 | Difficulty: Easy)
Per serving: Calories 240, Total fat 15g, Protein 23g, Carbs 2g

Ingredients:

- 1/2 pound (8 oz.) of salmon fillet
- 2 whole mangos, peeled, seeded & chopped
- 1/2 whole habanero pepper, seeded & chopped
- 1 whole cedar planks
- Olive oil
- 1/4 cup of lime juice
- 1 small finely diced cucumber
- 1/2 red onion, diced
- Salmon Shake
- 2 teaspoons of honey
- 1/4 tablespoon of finely chopped cilantro

Instructions:

- Whisk together the onion, mango, cucumber, lime juice, chili pepper, and honey inside a mixing bowl. Season with more lime juice, chili, or honey to taste. Fold in the cilantro gently. Cover and chill if not using immediately.
- Preheat your griddle at medium heat and coat it using a thin layer of oil.
- It's finally time to drain the plank. Season the salmon on all sides with olive oil and shake. Position the plank skin side up.
- Place the plank with the salmon directly on the griddle for around 25 to 30 minutes or till the salmon is opaque and flakes easily with a fork. Serve with mango salsa on the side. (The fish can be served on or off the plank.)

8. Seafood Ceviche

(Preparation time: 10 minutes | Cooking time: 1-hour | Servings: 4 | Difficulty: Easy)

Per serving: Calories 223, Total fat 2g, Protein 36g, Carbs 16g

Ingredients:

- 1 pound of shrimp, peeled & deveined
- 2 teaspoons of salt
- 1 pinch of red pepper flakes
- 1 pound of sea scallops, shucked

- 1 orange, juiced
- 1/2 red onion, diced
- 1 tablespoon of canola oil
- 1 tablespoon of cilantro, finely chopped
- 1 lime, zested & juiced
- 1 teaspoon of onion powder
- 1 lemon juice
- 1/2 teaspoon of black pepper
- 1 teaspoon of garlic powder
- 1 diced avocado

Instructions:

- Combine the shrimp, scallops, and canola oil inside a mixing bowl.
- Preheat your griddle at medium heat and coat it using a thin layer of oil.
- Cook the shrimp and scallops for about 45 minutes on the griddle. Prepare the remaining ingredients and combine them inside a large mixing bowl while the others are cooking.
- Raise the temperature at high and continue to cook the shrimp and scallops for 5 minutes more to ensure they are fully cooked.
- Allow the scallops and shrimp to cool before slicing them in half lengthwise and tossing them with the remaining ingredients.
- Chill the ceviche for at least 2-3 hours to allow the flavors to blend. With corn chips on the side, serve.

9. Roasted Stuffed Rainbow Trout with Brown Butter

(Preparation time: 10 minutes | Cooking time: 20 minutes | Servings: 2 | Difficulty: Easy)

Per serving: Calories 210, Total fat 4g, Protein 26g, Carbs 8g

Ingredients:

- 2 teaspoons of Chipotle pepper
- 4 whole oranges, sliced
- 2 whole rainbow trout, cleaned
- 8 tablespoons of butter
- 2 tablespoons of salt
- 6 whole bay leaves
- 2 cloves of garlic, chopped
- Lemon, juiced
- 8 sprig thyme sprigs

Instructions:

- Preheat your griddle at medium heat and coat it using a thin layer of oil.

- Melt the butter on the griddle inside a small-sized saucepan. When the butter has completely melted, it will foam, and the milk solids will begin to brown (keep an eye on it because it will happen quickly). Remove the pan from the griddle once the foam has subsided and the butter has turned golden brown. Squeeze in some lemon juice to slow the browning process. Place them aside.

- Make a piece of foil that is 3" (8cm) longer on each end than the fish. Season the fish with salt and chipotle powder after pouring the brown butter on the outside and cavities. Fold the foil into a package and fill the cavity with the remaining ingredients.

- Cook for about 15 minutes, or till the temperature reaches 145°F, with the package on the griddle. Enjoy!

10. Roasted Halibut with Tartar Sauce

(Preparation time: 10 minutes | Cooking time: 20 minutes | Servings: 2 | Difficulty: Easy)

Per serving: Calories 455, Total fat 14g, Protein 41g, Carbs 28g

Ingredients:

- 1 cup of mayonnaise
- 1/2 cup of chopped pickles
- 6 pieces of thick-cut halibut fillets
- 1/2 tablespoon of Dijon mustard
- Olive oil
- 1/2 tablespoon of chopped parsley
- 1 tablespoon of chopped capers
- 1/2 medium lemon, juiced
- Sea salt

Instructions:

- To allow the flavors to meld, make the tartar sauce at least an hour ahead of time. Combine mayonnaise, dill pickles, lemon juice, capers, and mustard inside a mixing bowl. Mix. Toss in the herbs and season using salt and pepper to taste.

- Preheat your griddle to medium-high heat and coat it with a thin layer of oil.

- Place the halibut fillets on a baking sheet. Pour in the olive oil, season with sea salt, and fully coat the fillets in it with your hands. Allow for a 5-minute break.

- Put the fillets on the griddle, presentation side up. Cook the fish on the griddle till it is opaque.

- Reduce the temperature to low and cook the salmon for another 3-5 minutes. On a serving plate, arrange the fish with lemon wedges and tartar sauce.

11. Oysters with Tequila Butter Skillet

(Preparation time: 10 minutes | Cooking time: 20 minutes | Servings: 6 | Difficulty: Medium)

Per serving: Calories 100, Total fat 2g, Protein 5g, Carbs 2g

Ingredients:

- 3 dozen scrubbed medium oysters
- 7 tablespoons of unsalted butter
- ½ teaspoon of fennel seeds
- 2 tablespoons of lemon juice
- Rock salt, for the serving
- ¼ teaspoon of crushed red pepper
- 36 small leaves for the garnishing
- 1 teaspoon of dried oregano
- Kosher salt, to taste
- ¼ cup of sage leaves, plus
- 2 tablespoons of tequila

Instructions:

- Preheat your griddle at medium heat.
- Toast the fennel seeds and smashed red pepper in a pan on the griddle for about 1 minute or till fragrant.
- Put the mixture in a mortar and leave it to cool. Grind the spices to a powder with a pestle, then transfer them to a dish.
- Melt 3 1/2 tablespoons butter on the griddle in the same pan till it turns dark brown, about two minutes.
- Cook for about 2 minutes after adding 1/4 cup of sage, stirring occasionally. In a serving dish, arrange the sage.
- Combine the butter and spices in a mixing bowl. Using the remaining sage leaves and butter. Set aside a portion for garnishing.

- In the mortar, crush the fried sage leaves with the pestle. Season the butter with salt and black pepper after adding the smashed sage, lemon juice, oregano, and tequila. Keep them at a comfortable temperature.
- Remove the top shells of the oysters and place them on the rock salt, being careful not to spill their liquid.
- Spray the griddle top using cooking spray.
- Cook the oysters for around 10 minutes on the griddle.
- Serve the oysters topped with the warm tequila sauce and a sage leaf.

12. Parsley Herbed Fish Stew

(Preparation time: 15 minutes | Cooking time: 30 minutes | Servings: 8 | Difficulty: Easy)

Per serving: Calories 104, Total fat 4g, Protein 11g, Carbs 6g

Ingredients:

- ¼ cup of chicken stock
- 2 tablespoons of butter
- ¼ cup of white wine
- 1 jar (28 oz.) Crushed Tomatoes
- ½ lb. of shrimp divined & cleaned
- 2 oz. of tomato paste
- ½ lb. of Clams
- 2 minced garlic cloves
- ¼ diced onion
- ½ lb. of halibut parsley bread

Instructions:

- Preheat your griddle at medium heat.
- Melt the butter on the griddle inside a Dutch oven. Cook the onion for 4 to 7 minutes.
- It's time to add the garlic now. Cook for one more minute.
- Stir in the tomato paste in the same pan. Cook till the color turns rusty crimson. Pour in the wine and stock. Cook for ten minutes in total. Bring the tomatoes to a simmer after adding them.
- Chop the halibut and place it in the Dutch oven with the remaining fish. Cover it with a lid and place it on the griddle.

- After seasoning with black salt and black pepper and setting aside, the cooking time should be 20 minutes. Serve with toast and garnished with chopped parsley. Enjoy!

13. Sweet Mustard Calamari

(Preparation time: 10 minutes | Cooking time: 20 minutes | Servings: 6 | Difficulty: Easy)

Per serving: Calories 60, Total fat 2g, Protein 2g, Carbs 9g

Ingredients:

- 2 tablespoons of finely chopped fresh oregano
- Pepper, ground
- ½ cup of olive oil
- 2 cups of milk
- Juice from 2 lemons
- Calamari, cleaned
- 4 teaspoons of sweet mustard
- Sauce as required
- ½ bunch of finely chopped parsley

Instructions:

- Clean the calamari thoroughly before slicing it into pieces.
- Cover and marinate the calamari in milk overnight inside a large-sized bowl.
- Drain the calamari thoroughly after removing them from the milk.
- Lightly brush them with olive oil.
- Combine mustard and the juice of two lemons inside a mixing bowl.
- Whip in the olive oil lightly while constantly stirring till all ingredients are well combined.
- Combine the oregano, salt, and pepper. Preheat your griddle at medium heat and coat it using a thin layer of oil.
- Cook the calamari for around 4-5 minutes per side or till it has a slight sear.
- Serve the calamari on a platter with the mustard sauce and chopped parsley.

14. Swordfish with Corn Salsa

(Preparation time: 10 minutes | Cooking time: 35 minutes | Servings: 4 | Difficulty: Easy)

Per serving: Calories 170, Total fat 6g, Protein 20g, Carbs 8g

Ingredients:

- 4 whole swordfish fillets
- Salt & pepper
- Olive oil as needed

For the corn salsa:

- 1 medium minced serrano pepper
- 1/3 cup of chopped cilantro
- 4 whole ears corn, husked
- 1 medium red onion, diced small
- Salt & pepper
- 1 1/2 cups of cherry tomatoes
- Olive oil
- 1 whole lime, juiced

Instructions:

- Preheat your griddle at medium heat and coat it with a thin layer of oil.
- Season the corn with salt and black pepper after spraying it with olive oil.
- The corn should be completely cooked and lightly browned after 12 to 15 minutes on the griddle. Allow to cool completely.
- After the corn has cooled, remove the kernels and place them inside a medium-sized bowl.
- Combine tomatoes, serrano peppers, cilantro, red onion, and lime juice inside a mixing bowl. Toss to combine and season with salt to taste.
- Season the fish steaks with salt and pepper after spraying them with olive oil. Cook the fish on the griddle for about 18 minutes or till opaque and flaky when pressed with a fork.
- Swordfish should be served with corn salsa. Enjoy!

15. Teriyaki Salmon

(Preparation time: 10 minutes | Cooking time: 10 minutes | Servings: 2 | Difficulty: Easy)

Per serving: Calories 270, Total fat 8g, Protein 47g, Carbs 3g

Ingredients:

- 4 cloves of garlic
- 1 tablespoon of minced ginger
- 2 whole oranges, juiced
- Toasted sesame seeds
- 1 tablespoon of sesame seeds
- 2 whole orange zest
- 1 cup of soy sauce
- 6 tablespoons of brown sugar
- Scallions, chopped
- 4 pieces (5 oz.) of salmon fillets

Instructions:

- Except for the sesame seeds and the fish, combine everything inside a saucepan. Bring to the boil over medium heat on the griddle, then reduce to a syrupy consistency (about a 50% reduction). Allow to cool.
- Marinate the sesame seeds and fish for about an hour.
- Bring the sauce to a boil after removing the fish from the marinade.
- Preheat your griddle at medium-high and coat it with a thin layer of oil.
- Place the salmon fillets, skin side up, on the griddle. Cook the salmon for 3 to 5 minutes on each side or till done to your liking, brushing it with the Teriyaki Sauce as needed.
- When the salmon is done to your liking, remove it from the griddle and top it with chopped scallions and toasted sesame seeds. Enjoy!

16. Mexican Shrimp

(Preparation time: 10 minutes | Cooking time: 10 minutes | Servings: 4 | Difficulty: Easy)

Per serving: Calories 242, Total fat 13g, Protein 26g, Carbs 6g

Ingredients:

- 1 lb. of shrimp, peeled & deveined

For the marinade:

- 3 tablespoons of lime juice
- 1/2 teaspoon of paprika
- 1/4 teaspoon of chili flakes
- 2 tablespoons of garlic, minced
- Salt & pepper to taste
- 1/2 teaspoon of chili powder
- 3 tablespoons of olive oil
- 1/2 teaspoon of ground cumin

Instructions:

- Combine the shrimp and marinade ingredients inside a mixing bowl and thoroughly mix. After covering with plastic wrap, place in the refrigerator for 30 minutes.
- Preheat the griddle at medium-high heat.
- Coat the griddle's surface with cooking spray.
- Thread the marinated shrimp onto skewers.
- On hot griddle, cook the skewers for about 4-5 minutes on each side.
- Take pleasure in your meal.

17. Citrusy Clams with Tomatoes & Chickpeas

(Preparation time: 15 minutes | Cooking time: 30 minutes | Servings: 6 | Difficulty: Medium)

Per serving: Calories 349, Total fat 13g, Protein 31g, Carbs 21g

Ingredients:

- 24 scrubbed littleneck clams
- 1 tablespoon of fresh lime juice
- 2 large chopped shallots
- 1 cup of cherry tomatoes
- 6 tablespoons of unsalted pieces of butter

- 1 cup of beer
- 4 thinly sliced garlic cloves
- 1 ½ oz. (42 g) of rinsed chickpeas
- 2 tablespoons of olive oil
- 1 tablespoon of tomato paste
- Kosher salt
- 4 country-style bread thick slices
- ½ cup of cilantro leaves
- 2 tablespoons of sambal oiled
- Lime wedges

Instructions:

- Preheat your griddle at medium heat. Melt 4 tablespoons butter inside a large-sized skillet on the griddle.
- Cook for 4 minutes, stirring frequently, or until the garlic and shallots are softened.
- Simmer, occasionally stirring, till the tomato paste has darkened to a brick-red rich color. Add the tomatoes & beer.
- Cook for about 4 minutes or till the beer is nearly half its original volume. After the clams, add the chickpeas and oiled sambal.
- Cover and cook till the clams open, which could take around 5 to 10 minutes, based on their size and temperature. Any clams that refuse to open should be discarded.
- In a separate bowl, combine the lime juice and remaining two tablespoons of butter.
- While the clams are cooking, brush the bread with the butter mixture and season using salt. Grill for 5 minutes or until light brown and crunchy.
- To serve, toss the toast with the clam mixture and cilantro. On the side, lime wedges are served.

18. White Wine Shrimp Scampi

(Preparation time: 10 minutes | Cooking time: 15 minutes | Servings: 4 | Difficulty: Easy)

Per serving: Calories 330, Total fat 41g, Protein 17g, Carbs 31g

Ingredients:

- ¼ cup of white wine, dry
- ½ tablespoon of garlic powder

- 1 lb. (454 g) of raw shrimp, tail on
- ½ cup of salted butter, melted
- 1 tablespoon of lemon juice
- ½ tablespoon of salt
- ½ tablespoon of chopped fresh garlic

Instructions:

- Preheat your griddle at medium heat.
- Combine the butter, garlic, wine, and juice inside a mixing bowl, then pour into the cast iron pan. Allow 4 minutes for the ingredients to meld.
- Place the shrimp on the cast iron pan after coating them with garlic and salt.
- Cook for about 10 minutes with the pan on the griddle.
- When the shrimp are hot, remove them from the griddle and serve.
- Enjoy.

19. Garlicky Salmon with Avocado Salsa

(Preparation time: 10 minutes | Cooking time: 20 minutes | Servings: 6 | Difficulty: Easy)
Per serving: Calories 335, Total fat 22g, Protein 35g, Carbs 6g

Ingredients:

- 1 chopped onion
- 4 cups of avocado, sliced into cubes
- 1 minced jalapeño pepper
- ¼ cup of chopped cilantro
- 1 tablespoon of lime juice
- 3 lbs. of salmon fillet Garlic
- 1 tablespoon of olive oil
- Salt and pepper to taste

Instructions:

- Season the salmon on both sides with garlic, salt, and black pepper.
- Preheat your griddle at medium-high heat and coat it using a thin layer of oil.
- Cook the salmon for around 8 to 10 minutes on each side on the griddle.

- While you're waiting, make the salsa by combining the remaining ingredients inside a mixing bowl.
- Serve the salmon with avocado salsa on the side.

20. Crab Cakes

(Preparation time: 10 minutes | Cooking time: 15 minutes | Servings: 6 | Difficulty: Easy)

Per serving: Calories 202, Total fat 8g, Protein 13g, Carbs 17g

Ingredients:

- 1 cup of breadcrumbs
- 1 egg
- 1 teaspoon of old bay seasoning
- 1 teaspoon of lemon juice
- 2 teaspoons of Dijon mustard
- 1 lb. of crab meat
- 1/3 cup of mayonnaise
- 1 tablespoon of parsley, chopped

Instructions:

- Combine all of the ingredients inside a mixing bowl and stir till well combined.
- Preheat the griddle at medium-high heat.
- Coat the griddle's surface using cooking spray.
- With the ingredients, form 6 patties and cook for 6 minutes on each side on a hot griddle.
- Take pleasure in your meal.

21. Oysters with Spiced Tequila Butter

(Preparation time: 10 minutes | Cooking time: 25 minutes | Servings: 6 | Difficulty: Easy)

Per serving: Calories 184, Total fat 15g, Protein 2g, Carbs 4g

Ingredients:

- 3 dozen medium oysters, scrubbed & shucked
- Flakey sea salt, for serving

For the butter:

- 2 tablespoons of freshly squeezed lemon juice
- 1 teaspoon of dried oregano
- 2 tablespoons of tequila Blanco, like Espolon
- 1/4 teaspoon of crushed red pepper
- 7 tablespoons of unsalted butter
- ¼ teaspoon of chili oil

Instructions:

- Combine all of the butter ingredients inside a small-sized mixing bowl and set aside.
- Preheat your griddle at high heat and coat the griddle with a thin layer of oil.
- On the griddle, cook the oysters for 4 to 5 minutes on each side.
- The oysters should be seasoned with salt flakes.
- Microwave the butter for 30 seconds, then drizzle it over the oysters on the plates.

22. Gremolata Swordfish Skewers

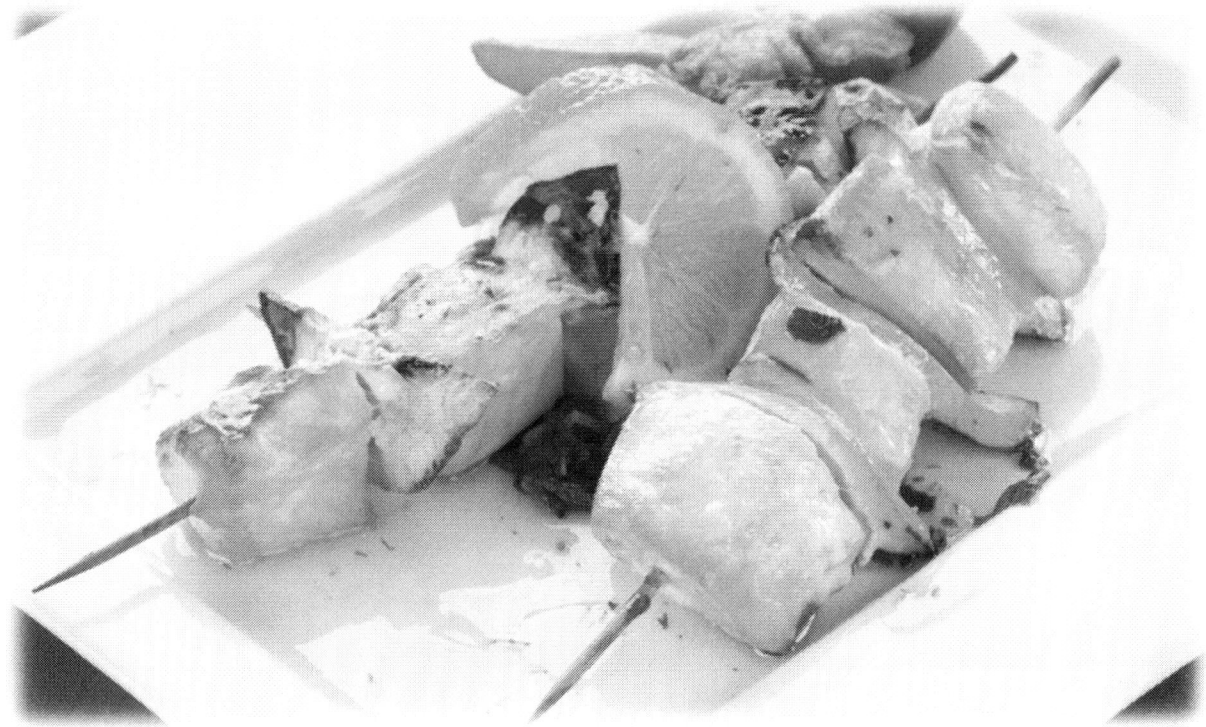

(Preparation time: 15 minutes | Cooking time: 15 minutes | Servings: 4 | Difficulty: Easy)

Per serving: Calories 333, Total fat 16g, Protein 44g, Carbs 3g

Ingredients:

- 3 tablespoons of lemon juice
- 1/2 teaspoon of red pepper flakes
- 2 teaspoons of garlic, minced
- 1 1/2 lbs. of skinless swordfish fillet
- 2 tablespoons of extra-virgin olive oil, plus extra for serving
- 1/2 cup of finely chopped parsley
- 3 lemons, cut into slices
- 1/4 teaspoon of black pepper
- 2 teaspoons of lemon zest
- 3/4 teaspoon of sea salt

Instructions:

- Preheat your griddle at medium-high heat and coat it with a thin layer of oil.
- Make the gremolata by combining lemon zest, parsley, garlic, 1/4 teaspoon salt, and pepper inside a small-sized bowl with a fork.
- Combine the swordfish, lemon juice, red pepper flakes, olive oil, and the remaining salt.
- Thread swordfish and lemon slices onto metal skewers alternately.
- Cook the skewers on the griddle for 8 to 10 minutes or until the fish is cooked through, flipping halfway through.
- On a serving plate, arrange the skewers with the gremolata.
- Drizzle with olive oil and serve.

23. Halibut Fillets with Spinach and Olives

(Preparation time: 10 minutes | Cooking time: 15 minutes | Servings: 4 | Difficulty: Easy)

Per serving: Calories 773, Total fat 37g, Protein 109g, Carbs 4g

Ingredients:

- 2 teaspoons of fresh dill, chopped
- 4 cups of baby spinach
- 1/3 cup of olive oil
- 4 (6 ounces) of halibut fillets
- Lemon wedges, to Servings
- 2 tablespoons of flat-leaf parsley, chopped
- 1/4 cup of lemon juice
- 2 ounces of pitted black olives, halved

Instructions:

- Preheat your griddle at medium-high heat and brush a thin layer of oil on top.
- Toss the spinach with the lemon juice inside a mixing bowl and set aside.
- Cook for around 3-4 minutes on each side or until the fish is cooked through, brushing with olive oil.
- Remove from the griddle and set aside for 5 minutes, covered.

- With the remaining oil, cook for about 2 minutes or until the spinach is slightly wilted. Take it off the griddle.
- After tossing with olives and herbs, transfer to serving plates with the fish and lemon wedges.

24. Tuna with Pistachio Sauce

(Preparation time: 15 minutes | Cooking time: 10 minutes | Servings: 4 | Difficulty: Medium)

Per serving: Calories 307, Total fat 12g, Protein 31g, Carbs 5g

Ingredients:

- 2 tablespoons of chopped pistachios
- 4 parsley leaves
- Salt & pepper to taste
- 21 oz. of tuna fillet
- ½ lemon
- 1 sprig of rosemary
- Olive oil as needed

Instructions:

- After washing and drying the tuna fillet, place it in a dish.
- The rosemary should be thoroughly washed and dried.
- Combine the rosemary, filtered lemon juice, oil, salt, and pepper in the same bowl as the tuna.
- Refrigerate the bowl for about 30 minutes, covered.
- Meanwhile, wash and dry the parsley.
- Combine the salt, chopped pistachios, parsley, oil, and pepper in the mixing glass.
- Using the mixer, blend the sauce till it is smooth and homogeneous.
- After 30 minutes, remove the tuna from the refrigerator.
- Preheat your griddle at medium heat.
- Spray the griddle top using cooking spray.
- On the griddle, cook the tuna for about 4 to 5 minutes on each side.

- After the tuna has finished cooking, remove it from the griddle, place it on a cutting board, and cut it into slices.
- To serve, arrange the tuna pieces on plates.
- Serve with a drizzle of pistachio sauce on top.

25. Halibut Fillets with Lemon and Butter Sauce

(Preparation time: 10 minutes | Cooking time: 20 minutes | Servings: 2 | Difficulty: Easy)

Per serving: Calories 224, Total fat 5g, Protein 25g, Carbs 8g

Ingredients:

- 4 thick-cut halibut fillets
- 2 tablespoons of unsalted butter
- Fin & Feather Rub

For the lemon and butter sauce:

- 1 small shallot, thinly diced
- 2 sprigs of fresh thyme
- 1/2 cup of white wine
- 1 teaspoon of kosher salt
- 1/2 teaspoon of freshly ground white pepper
- 1 stick of cubed unsalted butter
- 1/2 lemon, juiced
- 1 tablespoon of heavy cream

Instructions:

- Preheat your griddle at medium-high heat and coat it with a thin layer of oil.
- Inside a griddle-safe saucepan, combine the wine, thyme, shallots, and lemon juice. Reduce the mixture by half by bringing it to a low simmer on griddle.
- Stir in the heavy cream constantly. Add the butter in small increments, constantly beating with a wire whisk after each addition. The sauce should never boil, so constantly whisk it.
- Season using salt and black pepper to taste, and then strain through a fine-mesh strainer to remove any remaining particles. Return the strained sauce to the saucepan and keep warm till ready to serve.

- Fin & Feather Rub is used to season the halibut. In a hot cast iron pan, melt the butter on the griddle. Sear the halibut fillets in a skillet with the butter till they reach an internal temperature of 140°F, about 4-5 minutes per side.

- Remove the steaks from the griddle and serve with a side of warm lemon butter sauce. Enjoy!

Chapter 8: Poultry Recipes

1. Creole Chicken Stuffed with Cheese & Peppers

(Preparation time: 10 minutes | Cooking time: 20 minutes | Servings: 4 | Difficulty: Medium)

Per serving: Calories 509, Total fat 25g, Protein 51g, Carbs 20g

Ingredients:

- 2 slices of pepper jack cheese, cut in half
- 1 tablespoon of creole seasoning, like Emeril's
- 2 slices of Colby jack cheese, cut in half
- 1 teaspoon of black pepper
- 4 boneless and skinless chicken breasts
- 1 teaspoon of onion powder
- 8 mini sweet peppers, sliced thinly & seeded
- Toothpicks

- 4 teaspoons of olive oil, separated
- 1 teaspoon of garlic powder

Instructions:

- Rinse and pat the chicken dry.
- Combine garlic powder, creole seasoning, pepper, and onion powder inside a small-sized mixing bowl; set aside.
- Make a slit down the side of each chicken breast, but don't cut all the way through.
- Rub each chicken breast with 1 teaspoon of olive oil and coat evenly with the spice mixture.
- Stuff each chicken breast with half a pepper jack cheese slice, half a Colby cheese slice, and a handful of pepper pieces.
- Close the chicken with 4 or 5 toothpicks.
- Preheat your griddle to medium-high heat and spray the griddle top using cooking spray.
- Cook the chicken for around 8 to 10 minutes per side or until the internal temperature reaches 165°F.
- Set toothpicks aside for 5 minutes before serving.

2. Classical Chicken Meatballs in Hot Sauce

(Preparation time: 20 minutes | Cooking time: 20 minutes | Servings: 4 | Difficulty: Medium)

Per serving: Calories 300, Total fat 10g, Protein 22g, Carbs 15g

Ingredients:

- 1 egg
- 12 oz. of ground chicken meat
- 4 chopped parsley leaves
- Salt & pepper to taste
- 3 tablespoons of grated parmesan cheese
- Breadcrumb to taste

For the sauce:

- ½ chopped shallot
- Salt & pepper to taste
- 2 cups of hot sauce
- Olive oil to taste

Instructions:

- Preheat your griddle at medium heat.
- Inside a mixing bowl, combine the chicken meat, egg, salt, grated Parmesan cheese, parsley, and pepper.
- Knead the ingredients together using your hands till they are smooth and uniform.
- If it's too moist, add some breadcrumbs to adjust the consistency.
- Form the meatballs with wet hands.
- Form into normal balls and serve on a dish with breadcrumbs.
- Before chopping the half shallot, it should be peeled and washed.
- In a baking pan brushed with olive oil, combine the shallot, spicy sauce, and meatballs.
- Cook for about 20 minutes on the griddle with the baking pan, stirring frequently.
- When they're done, remove them from the griddle and set them aside for 5 minutes to rest.
- Serve immediately on serving plates, drizzled with the sauce.

3. Grilled Chicken with Fruit Salsa

(Preparation time: 20 minutes | Cooking time: 20 minutes | Servings: 4 | Difficulty: Easy)

Per serving: Calories 391, Total fat 12g, Protein 46g, Carbs 24g

Ingredients:

- 4 boneless and skinless chicken breasts

For the marinade:

- 1/2 cup of fresh lemon juice
- 1 tablespoon of fresh ginger, minced
- 2 garlic cloves, minced
- 1 tablespoon of lemon pepper seasoning

- 1/2 cup of soy sauce

For the salsa:

- ½ teaspoon of olive oil, more for brushing griddle
- 1 small jalapeño pepper, seeded & chopped
- 3/4 cup of kiwi fruit, chopped
- 1 1/2 cups of pineapple, chopped
- 2 tablespoons of fresh cilantro, chopped
- 1/8 teaspoon of black pepper
- 1 1/2 teaspoons of ground cumin
- 1/2 cup of red onion, finely chopped
- 1/2 cup of mango, chopped
- 1/4 teaspoon of sea salt

Instructions:

- Combine the marinade ingredients inside a large-sized sealable plastic bag.
- Close the bag and toss the chicken around in it to coat it.
- Refrigerate for 1 hour to allow the flavors to mingle.
- Combine all of the salsa ingredients inside a mixing bowl and gently toss to combine. Set aside till ready to use.
- Preheat your griddle at high heat.
- Take the chicken out of the bag and discard the marinade.
- On a griddle brushed with olive oil, cook the chicken for around 7 to 8 minutes on each side or till cooked through.
- Serve the chicken with salsa on top with your favorite side dishes.

4. Wild Duck Breast

(Preparation time: 10 minutes | Cooking time: 20 minutes | Servings: 4 | Difficulty: Easy)

Per serving: Calories 297, Total fat 11g, Protein 43g, Carbs 5g

Ingredients:

- 2 tablespoons of olive oil
- ½ teaspoon of hot sauce

- 4 skinned and boned duck breast halves
- ¼ cup of Worcestershire sauce
- 2 tablespoons of minced garlic
- ¼ teaspoon of black pepper

Instructions:

- Inside a large-sized bowl, mix together the Worcestershire sauce, hot sauce, olive oil, garlic, and pepper. Mix well to coat the duck breasts. Cover it and put it in the fridge for 30 minutes to a day.
- Preheat the griddle at medium heat and coat the griddle top using cooking spray.
- Take the duck out of the marinade and cook it on a hot griddle for 5 to 7 minutes per side or till it's done the way you like it. When a thermometer is put in the middle, it should show at least 165 degrees F. Discard marinade.

5. Turkey in Herb Sauce

(Preparation time: 15 minutes | Cooking time: 1 hour 15 minutes | Servings: 4 | Difficulty: Easy)

Per serving: Calories 190, Total fat 6g, Protein 28g, Carbs 7g

Ingredients:

- ¼ cup of milk
- 1 tablespoon of chopped chives
- 1 tablespoon of chopped rosemary
- 5 chopped sage leaves
- 1 sprig of chopped parsley
- Salt & red pepper to taste
- 1 clove of garlic
- Olive oil to taste
- 1 tablespoon of thyme leaves
- 1.5-pound of the whole turkey
- 1 shallot

Instructions:

- After washing and drying the turkey, brush it with olive oil and season it with salt and pepper.
- Before chopping the shallot and garlic, they should be peeled and washed.
- Pour the milk over the turkey into the roasting pan.
- Sprinkle all of the aromatic herbs over the surface of the turkey.
- Preheat your griddle at medium-high heat for about 15 minutes.
- Cook the turkey for around 75 minutes, or until the internal temperature reaches 185°F.
- When the roasting pan has finished cooking, remove it from the griddle and set it aside for 10 minutes.
- After cutting the turkey into pieces, arrange it on serving dishes.
- Serve with the cooking liquids on top.

6. Teriyaki Chicken and Veggie Rice Bowls

(Preparation time: 20 minutes | Cooking time: 20 minutes | Servings: 4 | Difficulty: Easy)

Per serving: Calories 477, Total fat 21g, Protein 26g, Carbs 48g

Ingredients:

- 1 bag of brown rice

For the skewers:

- 2 boneless and skinless chicken breasts, cubed
- 1 red onion, quartered
- 1/2 pineapple, cut into cubes
- 1 green pepper, cut into cube slices
- 1 red pepper, cut into cube slices

For the marinade:

- 1 tablespoon of ginger, fresh grated
- 1/4 cup of sesame oil
- 1/2 lime, juiced
- 1/4 cup of light soy sauce
- 1 garlic clove, crushed

Instructions:

- Combine the marinade ingredients inside a small-sized mixing bowl.
- Combine the chicken and marinade in a resealable plastic bag, seal, and toss to coat.
- Refrigerate for at least an hour but no more than 24 hours.
- Cook the rice according to the package directions.
- Preheat your griddle at medium-high heat.
- Spray the griddle top using cooking spray.
- Thread the chicken and vegetables onto eight metal skewers and grill for 8 minutes per side, or till browned and cooked through.
- To serve, spoon rice into bowls and top each with two skewers.

7. Tender & Sweet Chicken Skewers

(Preparation time: 10 minutes | Cooking time: 15 minutes | Servings: 6 | Difficulty: Easy)

Per serving: Calories 184, Total fat 8g, Protein 15g, Carbs 13g

Ingredients:

- 1 onion, chunks
- 2 chicken breasts, make bite-size pieces
- 1 bell pepper, chunks

For the marinade:

- 1 tablespoon of olive oil
- 3 tablespoons of soy sauce
- 1 teaspoon of minced ginger
- 3 tablespoons of honey
- 1 tablespoon of sesame oil
- 1 teaspoon of minced garlic

Instructions:

- Combine the chicken and marinade ingredients inside a mixing bowl and thoroughly mix. Allow approximately 1 hour for marinating.
- Thread the chicken, onion, and pepper onto skewers.
- Preheat the griddle at medium-high heat.
- Coat the griddle's surface using cooking spray.
- Cook for 10 minutes with skewers on a hot griddle. During cooking, skewers should be turned 2-3 times.
- Take pleasure in your meal.

8. Citrusy Goose Breast

(Preparation time: 20 minutes | Cooking time: 40 minutes | Servings: 8 | Difficulty: Easy)

Per serving: Calories 485, Total fat 32g, Protein 27g, Carbs 23g

Ingredients:

- ⅓ cup of Dijon mustard
- 1 tablespoon of dried minced onion
- ½ cup of orange juice
- ¼ cup of soy sauce
- 8 goose breast halves

- ⅓ cup of olive oil
- 1 teaspoon of garlic powder
- ⅓ cup of brown sugar
- ¼ cup of honey

Instructions:

- Marinate the goose for 3 to 6 hours in a mixture of orange juice, onion, honey, olive oil, soy sauce, mustard, sugar, and garlic powder that has been whisked together in a bowl.
- Preheat the griddle at medium heat.
- Position the goose breasts on a baking sheet.
- The goose breasts should be placed on the grill. For the very first 30 minutes, baste the meat with the marinade every so often before tossing it. Ten to fifteen minutes more of cooking time is required to achieve an internal temperature of the 165 degrees F (74 degrees C) and for the juices to run clear.

9. Moroccan Chicken

(Preparation time: 10 minutes | Cooking time: 15 minutes | Servings: 4 | Difficulty: Easy)
Per serving: Calories 401, Total fat 24g, Protein 43g, Carbs 4g

Ingredients:

- 2 tablespoons of lemon juice
- 1/2 teaspoon of ground cinnamon
- 4 chicken breasts, boneless & cut into 1-inch pieces
- 1/4 teaspoon of turmeric
- 1 tablespoon of garlic, minced
- 1/4 cup of olive oil
- Salt & pepper to taste
- 1 teaspoon of paprika
- 1 teaspoon of ground coriander
- 1 1/2 teaspoons of ground cumin
- 1 tablespoon of ginger, grated

Instructions:

- Combine the chicken and the remaining ingredients in a zip-lock bag.
- Refrigerate overnight after sealing and shaking the bag well.
- Preheat the griddle at medium-high heat.
- Coat the griddle's surface using cooking spray.
- On a hot griddle, cook the marinated chicken for about 5-7 minutes on each side.
- Take pleasure in your meal.

10. Chicken Satay in Almond Butter Sauce

(Preparation time: 20 minutes | Cooking time: 10 minutes | Servings: 4 | Difficulty: Medium)

Per serving: Calories 347, Total fat 20g, Protein 34g, Carbs 9g

Ingredients:

- 1 lb. Boneless and skinless chicken thighs, thin strips
- Olive oil, for the brushing

For the marinade:

- 1/2 teaspoon red chili flakes
- 1/2 cup light canned coconut milk
- 2 teaspoons grated ginger
- 1 tablespoon honey
- 1 1/2 teaspoons fish sauce
- 1/4 teaspoon ground coriander
- 1/2 lime, juiced
- 1 clove of grated garlic
- 2 teaspoons of soy sauce
- 1/2 teaspoon of curry powder

For the almond butter sauce:

- 1/2 teaspoon of low sodium soy sauce
- 1 tablespoon of honey
- 1/4 cup of the almond butter

- 1/2 teaspoon of Sriracha
- 1/4 cup of water
- 1 teaspoon of fresh grated ginger
- 2 tablespoons of canned light coconut milk
- 1/2 lime, juiced
- 1 teaspoon of fish sauce

Instructions:

- Combine all of the marinade ingredients inside a medium-sized mixing bowl.
- To coat the chicken, toss it inside the mixing bowl.
- Refrigerate, covered, for 2 hours or overnight.
- Brush the griddle using olive oil and heat it on medium-high.
- Thread the strips of chicken onto metal skewers.
- Cook the chicken skewers on the heated griddle for about 3 minutes, then rotate and cook for another 4 minutes or till the chicken is cooked through.
- Combine all of the ingredients for the almond butter sauce inside a small-sized saucepan on the griddle.
- Bring the sauce to the boil, then reduce to medium-low and cook for 1 to 2 minutes or till the sauce thickens.
- Enjoy the succulent chicken satay with almond butter sauce.

11. Goose and Kraut

(Preparation time: 20 minutes | Cooking time: 5 hours | Servings: 10 | Difficulty: Easy)

Per serving: Calories 565, Total fat 32g, Protein 73g, Carbs 24g

Ingredients:

- 2 (32-ounces) jars of sauerkraut with liquid
- 1 (10-pounds) of skinned and whole goose
- ¼ cup of brown sugar
- 2 cups of shredded potatoes
- 2 cups of applesauce

Instructions:

- Preheat the griddle at medium heat.
- Scrub the inside of the goose's cavity with cold running water. Use a paring knife to pierce the goose all over. Cover loosely using aluminum foil and place breast-side up on a broiler pan or roasting rack.
- Put on the griddle and cook for about an hour or till very tender. Take away from the griddle and wait for it to cool.
- To make this dish, place the shredded potatoes, applesauce, sauerkraut, and brown sugar inside a slow cooker on the griddle. Take out as much meat as you can from the goose, but leave it in chunks. Put them into the slow cooker with the other ingredients. Cook, covered, on HIGH for around 3 to 4 hours on the griddle.

12. BBQ Chili Smoked Turkey Breast

(Preparation time: 20 minutes | Cooking time: 2 hours | Servings: 8 | Difficulty: Medium)

Per serving: Calories 290, Total fat 6g, Protein 63g, Carbs 4g

Ingredients:

- Turkey breast (around 3-lbs., 1.4-kg.)

For the Rub:

- ¾ teaspoon of salt
- ½ teaspoon of pepper

For the Glaze:

- ¾ cup of ketchup
- 1 tablespoon of smoked paprika
- 3 tablespoons of white vinegar
- ¾ teaspoon of chili powder
- 1 tablespoon of olive oil
- ¼ teaspoon of cayenne powder
- 3 tablespoons of brown sugar

Instructions:

- Season your turkey breast with salt and black pepper in several places.
- Allow 10 minutes for the seasoned turkey breast to rest.
- Preheat your griddle at low-medium heat. Brush the griddle using a thin layer of oil.

- Cook the seasoned turkey breast on the griddle for about 1 hour.
- Meanwhile, on the other side of your griddle, inside a small-sized saucepan, combine the olive oil, garlic powder, ketchup, brown sugar, white vinegar, smoked paprika, chili powder, and cayenne pepper. Allow for a few minutes of boiling.
- After 1 hour, baste the turkey breast with the sauce and cook for an additional 1 hour.
- When the internal temperature of the turkey breast reaches 170°F, remove it from the griddle and cover it with aluminum foil.
- Allow the turkey breast to settle for 15 to 30 minutes before unwrapping it.
- Before serving, cut the smoked turkey breast into thick slices.

13. Maple Bourbon Turkey

(Preparation time: 10 minutes | Cooking time: 3 hours | Servings: 8 | Difficulty: Medium)
Per serving: Calories 536, Total fat 20g, Protein 56g, Carbs 24g
Ingredients:

- 1 tablespoon of minced rosemary
- 2 garlic cloves (minced)
- 1 teaspoon of salt
- 1 teaspoon of paprika
- 1 orange (wedged)
- 1 stick of butter (softened)
- 1 apple (wedged)
- 1 teaspoon of pepper
- 1 teaspoon of thyme
- 1 onion
- 8 cups of chicken broth
- 1 teaspoon of dried basil
- 1 (12 pounds) of turkey
- 1 lemon (wedged)

For the Maple Bourbon Glaze:

- 1 tablespoon of lime

- 1/2 cup of maple syrup
- 1 stick of butter (melted)
- ¾ cup of bourbon

Instructions:

- Wash the inside and outside of all the turkey meat underneath cold running water.
- Put the apple, lemon, orange, and onion inside the turkey.
- Inside a bowl, mix together the garlic, butter, paprika, thyme, pepper, basil, salt, and rosemary.
- Coat the turkey with the herb butter mixture.
- Place a rack and the turkey on the rack in a roasting pan. Pour a cup of chicken broth into the bottom of the roasting pan.
- Warm up your griddle for about 15 minutes at medium until it reaches 350°F.
- Use the roasting pan to cook on the griddle for an hour.
- Mix all of the ingredients for the maple bourbon glaze together inside a bowl. Mix everything together till it's well mixed.
- Coat the turkey with the glaze mixture. Cook the turkey for another hour, basting it every 30 minutes and adding more broth as needed or till the temperature inside reaches 165°F.
- After you take the turkey off the griddle, let it sit for a few minutes. Cut it into pieces and serve.

14. Stuffed Gouda Chicken Meatloaf

(Preparation time: 20 minutes | Cooking time: 50 minutes | Servings: 4 | Difficulty: Easy)

Per serving: Calories 360, Total fat 10g, Protein 35g, Carbs 30g

Ingredients:

- 3 tablespoons of breadcrumbs
- 1/2 cup of gouda cheese
- 10 oz. of ground chicken
- Olive oil to taste
- Salt and pepper to taste
- 1 yolk

- ½ glass of milk

Instructions:

- Set your griddle at medium until it reaches 300°F.
- Spray the griddle top using cooking spray.
- Half-fill a bowl with ground meat.
- Mix the egg yolk in with a spoon, and then add the breadcrumbs in small amounts. If the mixture is too dry, add milk until it is soft and even.
- Add the salt and pepper and stir again.
- Then, add the cubed Gouda cheese and shape the meatloaf into a tube.
- Roll it up tight and wrap it in aluminum foil.
- Put the meatloaf on the griddle and cook it for around 50 minutes.
- Take the roll off the griddle and wait 10 minutes before taking off the foil.
- Cut the meatloaf into slices and put them on plates to serve.

15. Pears and Pine Nuts Stuffed Chicken

(Preparation time: 20 minutes | Cooking time: 55 minutes | Servings: 4 | Difficulty: Medium)

Per serving: Calories 240, Total fat 10g, Protein 19g, Carbs 11g

Ingredients:

- 14 oz. of chicken breast
- 2 tablespoons of butter
- ½ glass of white wine
- Olive oil to taste
- 2 sage leaves
- 1 pear
- 2 tablespoons of pine nuts
- 1 tablespoon of grated Parmesan cheese
- Salt & pepper to taste

Instructions:

- To start, wash and dry the chicken meat. If there is any extra fat or bones, remove them.

- To get one slice, cut the chicken breast in half without separating the two pieces.
- Use the meat tenderizer to make it even more fine.
- Peel and wash pears before cutting them into thin slices.
- Sage needs to be cleaned and dried before it can be chopped.
- Add salt and pepper to the meat and put it on a cut.
- Put the pear, chopped sage, pine nuts, pieces of butter, and Parmesan cheese inside the meat.
- Wrap the meat securely using kitchen twine.
- Put the chicken rolls in an olive oil-brushed roasting pan.
- After putting oil on the meat, season it with salt and pepper. Then pour some white wine over the meat.
- Preheat your griddle at medium until it reaches 356°F.
- Put the roasting pan on the griddle and cook for about 55 minutes.
- If the chicken's core temperature is 176°F, take it off the griddle. If it's not at that temperature, cook for another 10 minutes.
- When it's done, take it off the griddle and set it aside for 15 minutes.
- After taking out the kitchen thread, cut the rolls into pieces.
- Pour the cooking liquids over the food on the plates.

16. Duck with Soy, Honey, and Ginger

(Preparation time: 20 minutes | Cooking time: 30 minutes | Servings: 2 | Difficulty: Easy)

Per serving: Calories 260, Total fat 9g, Protein 21g, Carbs 20g

Ingredients:

- 1 pinch of cayenne pepper
- 2 duck breast halves
- 1 pinch of salt
- 1 tablespoon of grated fresh ginger
- 1 pinch of ground black pepper
- ½ cup of chicken stock
- 2 tablespoons of honey

- 1 pinch of chili powder
- 2 tablespoons of soy sauce
- 1 tablespoon of tomato sauce
- 2 tablespoons of rice wine
- 1 teaspoon of lime juice

Instructions:

- Preheat the griddle at medium heat.
- Score the duck breasts four times across the skin and fat, but only just to the meat, using a sharp knife. Season the skin using salt, cayenne pepper, and black pepper.
- Heat ovenproof skillet on the griddle. Place the breasts inside the skillet skin-side down and cook for 5 minutes or till the skin is brown and crisp. Remove any extra fat out from the bottom of the skillet with a spoon. Cook for around 1 minute on the other side.
- Roast till the internal temperature of the widest part of the breasts reaches 160°F for well done, or the breasts attain the desired doneness.
- Cover the duck breasts using foil after removing them from the skillet. Set aside to cool. Remove any extra fat from skillet. In a skillet on the griddle, combine the stock, chili powder, honey, soy sauce, tomato sauce, rice wine, ginger, and lime juice. Whisk the sauce, bring to the boil, and cook till the sauce thickens, around 2 minutes. Slice duck breasts thinly, position them on the serving plates, and drizzle using the sauce.

17. Turkey Breast Noodles with Ginger and Parsley

(Preparation time: 10 minutes | Cooking time: 15 minutes | Servings: 4 | Difficulty: Medium)

Per serving: Calories 350, Total fat 7g, Protein 28g, Carbs 23g

Ingredients:

- 2 tablespoons of chopped parsley
- 7 oz. of noodles
- 2 cloves of garlic
- 4 tablespoons of soy sauce
- Salt & pepper to taste
- 1 turkey breast of 21 oz.
- 2 tablespoons of grated ginger

- Olive oil to taste

Instructions:

- After you wash and dry the turkey, put it in a dish.
- Before they are chopped, garlic cloves should be peeled and washed.
- Before chopping parsley, it should be washed and dried.
- Mix the turkey with the garlic, parsley, salt, soy sauce, oil, and pepper inside a bowl. Mix all the ingredients together well.
- Cover the bowl with cling film and put it in the fridge for 2 hours.
- Set your griddle at medium-high for about 15 minutes.
- Spray the griddle top using cooking spray.
- Put the turkey on the griddle and cook it for about 15 minutes.
- After the turkey has been turned once, brush it with the marinade.
- In the meantime, boil water in a bowl and cook the noodles for 10 minutes.
- After the turkey is done cooking, take it off the griddle and let it rest for 10 minutes.
- Put the noodles on the plates that will be used to serve.
- Put the turkey slices on top of the noodles.
- Pour some oil on top and add some soy sauce.

18. Cumin Spiced Turkey Breast

(Preparation time: 10 minutes | Cooking time: 2 hours | Servings: 6 | Difficulty: Easy)
Per serving: Calories 344, Total fat 12g, Protein 29g, Carbs 9g

Ingredients:

For the Brine:

- 4 cups of cold water
- 1 cup of brown sugar
- 2 tablespoons of ground black pepper
- ¼ cup of salt
- 2 pounds (907g) of turkey breast, deboned

For the BBQ Rub:

- 2 tablespoons of garlic powder
- 2 tablespoons of brown sugar
- 1 tablespoon of cayenne pepper
- 2 tablespoons of dried onions
- 2 tablespoons of sugar
- ¼ cup of paprika
- 2 tablespoons of ground black pepper
- 2 tablespoons of ground cumin
- 1 tablespoon of salt
- 2 tablespoons of red chili powder

Instructions:

- Mix black pepper, salt, and sugar inside a large-sized mixing bowl. Add water and stir till the sugar is dissolved.
- Put the turkey breast in it, cover it, and put it in the fridge for about 12 hours.
- Make the BBQ rub by putting all of the ingredients inside a small-sized bowl and stirring them together till they are well mixed. Set aside till needed.
- Then take the turkey breast out of the brine and use a lot of the BBQ rub you made to season it.
- Heat the griddle at low heat and coat it with a thin layer of oil.
- Put the turkey breast on the griddle and cook it for about 1 to 2 hours.
- Move the turkey to a cutting board and set it aside for 10 minutes before slicing and serving.

19. Roasted Duck

(Preparation time: 10 minutes | Cooking time: 2 hours 10 minutes | Servings: 4 | Difficulty: Easy)

Per serving: Calories 625, Total fat 45g, Protein 52g, Carbs 2g

Ingredients:

- 1 (5-pounds) whole duck
- 2 teaspoons of paprika
- 1 teaspoon of black pepper
- ½ cup of melted butter, divided
- 2 teaspoons of salt

Instructions:

- Preheat the griddle at medium heat.
- Inside a small-sized bowl, combine salt, paprika, and pepper; rub the spice mixture onto duck skin. Inside a roasting pan, place the duck.
- Transfer the roasting pan on the griddle.

- Cook for around 45 minutes more after spooning 1/4 cup of melted butter over the duck.
- Spoon the remaining 1/4 cup of melted butter on the duck. Cook till golden brown, around 15 minutes more.

20. Sweet Mesquite Seasoned Chicken Breasts

(Preparation time: 10 minutes | Cooking time: 30 minutes | Servings: 4 | Difficulty: Easy)

Per serving: Calories 173, Total fat 16g, Protein 21g, Carbs 14g

Ingredients:

- 1 tablespoon of sweet mesquite seasoning
- 2 tablespoons of honey bourbon BBQ sauce
- 1 tablespoon of Worcestershire sauce
- 2 tablespoons of spicy BBQ sauce
- 1 teaspoon of garlic, crushed
- 4 chicken breasts
- ¼ cup of olive oil
- 2 tablespoons of regular BBQ sauce

Instructions:

- Preheat your griddle at medium heat and spread a thin layer of oil on it.
- Inside a large-sized bowl, mix together the garlic, oil, Worcestershire sauce, and mesquite flavor.
- Spread the spice mixture all over the chicken breasts.
- The chicken breasts should cook on the griddle for about 20 to 30 minutes.
- In the meantime, mix all three BBQ sauces together in a bowl.
- In the last 4–5 minutes of cooking, use the BBQ sauce mixture to coat the chicken breasts.
- Serve right away.

21. Apple, Rocket, and Pistachio Grilled Chicken

(Preparation time: 10 minutes | Cooking time: 50 minutes | Servings: 4 | Difficulty: Medium)

Per serving: Calories 310, Total fat 14g, Protein 29g, Carbs 11g

Ingredients:

- 2 tablespoons of chopped pistachios
- ½ cup of red wine
- 1 chicken breast of 21 oz.
- 3 sprigs of rosemary
- Salt and pepper to taste
- 1 red apple
- Olive oil to taste
- 3 tablespoons of apple cider vinegar
- 1/4 cup of rocket

Instructions:

- First, wash and dry the chicken breasts.
- You should wash and dry the rosemary.
- Put the chicken in an oil-brushed roasting pan.
- Sprinkle with oil, then season with salt and pepper and a splash of red wine.
- Add the rosemary as well.
- Heat up your griddle for about 15 minutes at medium heat.
- Give the chicken breasts about 50 minutes to cook.
- After the roast is done cooking, take it off the griddle and let it rest for 10 minutes.
- Inside a bowl, mix the oil, salt, and pepper together.
- Before putting the rocket in bowls to serve, it should be washed and dried.
- After you peel and wash the apple, take out all of the seeds in the middle.
- Cut the apple into cubes with a knife.
- Put the apple cubes and rockets on plates to serve.
- Cut up the roast and serve it with the apple and rocket.

- Top with chopped pistachios and a pistachio emulsion.

22. Lemon Ginger Chicken with Fruit Salsa

(Preparation time: 10 minutes | Cooking time: 25 minutes | Servings: 3 | Difficulty: Medium)

Per serving: Calories 479, Total fat 26g, Protein 45g, Carbs 16g

Ingredients:

- 3 boneless chicken breast halves
- 1 cup of strawberries, sliced
- Sea salt for seasoning
- 1/4 cup of poppy seed dressing, plus ½ cup for basting chicken
- Black pepper, for seasoning
- 1 cup of fresh blueberries, rinsed
- 1 bag (8 oz.) of romaine salad
- 1/4 cup of almonds, sliced

Instructions:

- Put 1/2 cup of poppy seed dressing on the chicken and baste it. Season each chicken breast with a pinch of pepper and sea salt.
- Set your griddle to a temperature between medium-high and high.
- Spray the griddle top using cooking spray.
- Grill the chicken for about 10 minutes per side, or till the middle is no longer pink, brushing it with more poppy seed dressing as needed.
- Give the chicken a five-minute break.
- Mix the lettuce mix with the 1/4 cup of dressing that is left.
- Put the salad in three bowls and top each one with the same number of blueberries and strawberries.
- Chicken should be cut across the grain into slices that are 1/2 inch thick.
- To serve, put one sliced chicken breast and some almonds in each salad bowl.

23. Duck Adobo

(Preparation time: 20 minutes | Cooking time: 2 hours 20 minutes | Servings: 6 | Difficulty: Medium)

Per serving: Calories 111, Total fat 5g, Protein 11g, Carbs 7g

Ingredients:

- ½ cup of soy sauce
- 6 duck legs
- 1 large sliced onion
- 8 cloves of minced garlic
- 1 cup of seasoned rice vinegar
- 2 teaspoons OF sambal chili paste or any other hot pepper sauce
- 1 ½ cups of chicken broth
- Salt & ground black pepper to taste
- 2 bay leaves
- 1 tablespoon of vegetable oil

Instructions:

- Season the duck legs using salt & pepper.
- Preheat the griddle at medium heat.
- Inside a large-sized, deep skillet on the griddle, heat the vegetable oil; add the duck legs, skin side down, & cook till browned, around 3 to 4 minutes on each side. Remove the duck legs from the pan and drain all but one tablespoon of the duck fat.
- Cook the onion in the reserved duck fat for 3 to 4 minutes or till it begins to turn translucent. Cook and stir garlic for 1 to 2 minutes or till fragrant.
- Simmer the onion mixture with the soy sauce, chicken broth, sambal chili paste, rice vinegar, and bay leaves. Return the duck legs to the skillet on the griddle, cover loosely, and cook till tender and smoothly pierced using a fork, approximately 2 hours.
- Remove the cover from the skillet and cook till the sauce thickens, around 5 minutes; season using salt & black pepper to taste.

24. Smoked Marinated Turkey Breast

(Preparation time: 15 minutes | Cooking time: 3 hours | Servings: 6 | Difficulty: Medium)

Per serving: Calories 703, Total fat 34g, Protein 131g, Carbs 10g

Ingredients:

- 1 (around 5 pounds) of boneless chicken breast
- 2 tablespoons of kosher salt
- 4 cups of water
- 1 tablespoon of cider vinegar
- 2 tablespoons of honey
- 1 teaspoon of Italian seasoning

For the Rub:

- 1 teaspoon of oregano
- ½ teaspoon of garlic powder
- 1 teaspoon of paprika
- 1 tablespoon of brown sugar
- ½ teaspoon of onion powder
- 1 teaspoon of salt
- 1 teaspoon of ground black pepper

Instructions:

- Inside a large-sized container, mix the water, Italian spice, honey, cider vinegar, and salt.
- Add the chicken breasts and stir them around. Cover the bowl with plastic wrap and put it in the fridge for about 4 hours.
- Rinse the chicken breasts in water and pat them dry using paper towels to clean them.
- Inside a separate bowl, mix the brown sugar, onion powder, salt, paprika, oregano, pepper, and garlic.
- Season the turkey breasts well using the rub mixture.
- Warm up your griddle for about 15 minutes at low-medium heat.
- Put the turkey breasts on a griddle rack and position the griddle rack on your griddle.
- The turkey breast should be cooked for about 2 to 3 hours or till the temperature inside reaches 165°F.
- Take the chicken breasts off the griddle and put them somewhere else to cool down. Serve, and have fun.

25. Wine and Thyme Turkey Stew

(Preparation time: 20 minutes | Cooking time: 40 minutes | Servings: 4 | Difficulty: Easy)

Per serving: Calories 320, Total fat 2g, Protein 25g, Carbs 4g

Ingredients:

- 1 cup of red wine
- 2 sage leaves
- 1 turkey breast of 21 oz.
- Flour to taste
- 2 thyme sprigs
- Salt and pepper to taste
- ½ cup of tomato sauce
- Olive oil to taste

Instructions:

- Preheat your griddle at medium heat for about 15 minutes.
- Before chopping, the thyme and sage should be washed and dried.
- Before cutting the turkey breast into cubes, it should be washed and dried.
- Mix the turkey cubes with the flour and set them aside.
- Put two tablespoons of olive oil inside a high-sided skillet on the griddle and cook the sage and thyme for two minutes.
- Now, add the turkey and cook it for about 3 minutes while stirring constantly.
- After adding salt and pepper, add the red wine and tomato purée.
- Cook for about 30 minutes, stirring every now and then and keeping the lid on the pan.
- When the time is up, take the saucepan off the griddle and stir it a few times.
- Let the stew sit for 5 minutes before putting it on a plate and serving it.

Chapter 9: Beef, Pork, and Lamb Recipes

1. Beef Steak with Curry Sauce and Pine Nuts

(Preparation time: 20 minutes | Cooking time: 25 minutes | Servings: 4 | Difficulty: Medium)

Per serving: Calories 424, Total fat 27g, Protein 44g, Carbs 2g

Ingredients:

- 4 beef steaks (5.2 oz. each)
- 1 tablespoon of pine nuts
- Olive oil to taste
- 2 shallots
- 1 teaspoon of curry powder
- 2 tablespoons of milk
- Salt & pepper to taste
- 4 tablespoons of butter

- 1 glass of vegetable broth
- 2 teaspoons of chopped chives

Instructions:

- The steaks should be washed and dried to get rid of any extra fat.
- Peel and wash the shallots before cutting them into thin slices.
- Salt and black pepper are used to season the steaks after they have been brushed with olive oil.
- Preheat your griddle at medium-high temperature.
- Place the steaks on the griddle and cook for about 8 to 10 minutes per side, or till the internal temperature reaches 131°F.
- After grilling the steaks, take them off the griddle and put them on a plate. On the griddle put the pan so it can heat up for a few minutes.
- Once the butter has melted, add the shallots and cook for 5 minutes.
- Mix the broth, milk, and curry together.
- Season with salt and black pepper and bring to a boil. Then add the pine nuts.
- When the food is done cooking, take the pan off the griddle.
- Place the steaks on plates and pour the pine nut and curry sauce on top.
- Serve with chives on top.

2. Roast Beef Stuffed with Spinach and Speck

(Preparation time: 25 minutes | Cooking time: 50 minutes | Servings: 6 | Difficulty: Medium)

Per serving: Calories 348, Total fat 16g, Protein 51g, Carbs 7g

Ingredients:

- 21 oz. of fresh spinach
- 4 oz. of thinly sliced speck
- 1 glass of white wine
- Salt & pepper to taste
- 28 oz. of beef rump
- Olive oil to taste
- 4 tablespoons of grated Parmesan cheese

Instructions:

- After you wash the spinach, drain it.
- Preheat your griddle at medium heat.
- Heat up a pan by putting it on the griddle.
- When it is hot, heat a tablespoon of olive oil.
- When the oil is hot, cook the spinach for about 5 minutes.
- After adding salt and pepper, take the pan off the griddle and stir it.
- Wash and dry the meat, then cut off any extra fat before opening it like a book.
- First, put the spinach inside the meat, then the pieces of speck, and then the Parmesan cheese.
- Roll the meat in on itself, and then tie it shut with kitchen twine.
- Mix the wine, salt, olive oil, and pepper together inside a bowl.
- Brush the meat with the emulsion, then put it on the griddle after coating the griddle top using cooking spray.
- Using the temperature probe stuck into the center of the meat, cook for about 45 minutes or until the meat reaches 135°F.
- After the roast is done cooking, take it off the griddle and let it rest for 15 minutes.
- After 15 minutes, cut it into slices, put them on plates, and serve.

3. Grilled Ranch Pork Chops with Peach Jalapeno Salsa

(Preparation time: 10 minutes | Cooking time: 25 minutes | Servings: 6 | Difficulty: Easy)

Per serving: Calories 152, Total fat 6g, Protein 19g, Carbs 4g

Ingredients:

- 2 teaspoons of Salad Dressing & Seasoning Mix
- 4 bone-in pork chops, around 1-inch thick
- ½ jalapeno, minced
- Fresh lime juice, to taste
- ½ cup of diced red onion
- Kosher salt & freshly ground black pepper, to taste
- 1 ½ cups of diced peaches

Instructions:

- Preheat your griddle at medium and spread a thin layer of oil on it.
- Mix the peaches, red onion, and jalapeno together inside a small-sized bowl. Add the juice of at least half a lime. Salt and pepper can be added to taste. Take that into account.
- Use black pepper, ranch salad dressing, and seasoning. To add flavor to the pork chops, mix.
- Sear the chops for about 2 to 3 minutes on each side on the hot part of the griddle. Cook for another 6 to 8 minutes or till a thermometer reads 145°F. Put a dollop of salsa on top before serving.

4. Moroccan Spiced Pork Tenderloin with Creamy Harissa Sauce

(Preparation time: 20 minutes | Cooking time: 25 minutes | Servings: 6 | Difficulty: Easy)

Per serving: Calories 376, Total fat 18g, Protein 49g, Carbs 3g

Ingredients:

- 1 teaspoon of ground cilantro
- 1 teaspoon of ground cinnamon
- 2 (1 lb.) of pork tenderloins
- 1 teaspoon of sea salt
- 2 tablespoons of olive oil
- 1 teaspoon of paprika
- 1 teaspoon of ground cumin

For Creamy Harissa Sauce:

- 1 cup of Greek yogurt (8 ounces)
- 1 tablespoon of extra-virgin olive oil
- 1 tablespoon of fresh lemon juice
- Kosher salt & cracked black pepper
- 1 clove of garlic, minced
- 1 teaspoon of harissa sauce

Instructions:

- Mix all of the harissa's ingredients together inside a small-sized bowl and set it aside.
- Mix together cinnamon, coriander, salt, cumin, paprika, and olive oil.

- Spread the seasonings evenly on the pork tenderloins, then cover and put them in the fridge for about 30 minutes.

- Warm up the griddle over high heat and spread a thin layer of oil on it.

- Cook the tenderloins for 8 to 10 minutes or until they are browned.

- On the other side, cook for another 8 to 10 minutes. Place the tenderloins on a cutting board and cover them with foil. Set them aside for 10 minutes.

- Slice and serve with a side of creamy harissa sauce.

5. Lamb Lollipops with Mango Chutney

(Preparation time: 15 minutes | Cooking time: 15 minutes | Servings: 4 | Difficulty: Medium)

Per serving: Calories 286, Total fat 5g, Protein 38g, Carbs 18g

Ingredients:

- 3 cloves of chopped garlic
- 6 whole of lamb chops, around 3/4 thick, frenched
- 1 whole mango, peeled, seeded & chopped

- 2 tablespoons of chopped mint
- 1/2 tablespoon of coarse salt
- 1 teaspoon of salt
- 1/2 whole habanero pepper, seeded & chopped
- 2 tablespoons of olive oil
- 1 tablespoon of lime juice
- 3 sprigs of cilantro, finely chopped
- 1/2 teaspoon of cracked black pepper

Instructions:

- If you can't find frenched lamb chops, cut and scrape the meat and fat off the bone with a sharp knife to make it look like a lollipop.
- Put all of the chutney ingredients inside a food processor and pulse 15 times or till the consistency you want is reached. Set aside. Mint should be cut up and put in its own container.
- Preheat your griddle at medium-high heat and spread a thin layer of oil on it.
- While the griddle is getting hot, put the lamb lollipops on a baking sheet and brush them using olive oil. The coating needs to be put on both sides. Salt and black pepper on both sides then set aside at room temperature for 5 to 10 minutes.
- Put the poppers made with lamb on the griddle. On the griddle, cook for about 5 minutes. Cook for another 3 minutes on the other side or till a thermometer placed in the thickest part of the meat shows an internal temperature of 130°F.
- Before you serve them, take them off the griddle and set them aside for about 10 minutes to rest.
- On top of each lamb lollipop, you should sprinkle fresh-cut mint and spoon on the chutney. Enjoy!

6. Roasted Lamb with Root Vegetables

(Preparation time: 15 minutes | Cooking time: 1 hour 50 minutes | Servings: 8 | Difficulty: Medium)

Per serving: Calories 927, Total fat 39g, Protein 49g, Carbs 56g

Ingredients:

- 5 cloves of garlic, minced
- 1 bay leaf, crushed
- 8 carrots, peeled & trimmed
- 1 large beet, peeled & cut into wedges
- 2 tablespoons of balsamic vinegar
- 1 teaspoon of crushed red pepper flakes
- 16 small potatoes, unpeeled
- 1 (around 6 pounds) leg of lamb
- 8 baby turnips, peeled
- 2 teaspoons of coarsely ground black pepper
- ½ cup of olive oil
- 2 tablespoons of olive oil
- Salt to taste
- 1 tablespoon of chopped fresh rosemary
- 2 tablespoons of honey
- 1 yam, peeled & cut into wedges
- 2 tablespoons of coarse salt, or as needed

Instructions:

- Let the leg of lamb rest for an hour at room temperature before cooking it.
- Set your griddle at 400°F to heat it up.
- Inside a small-sized bowl, mix together the garlic, pepper, rosemary, red pepper flakes, bay leaf, vinegar, 1/2 cup olive oil, and honey. After spreading the mixture on the lamb, use 2 teaspoons of coarse salt to season it. Put them away. Inside a large roasting pan, mix together the carrots, yams, potatoes, beets, and turnips. Mix together two tablespoons of olive oil and a little bit of salt. Put the lamb leg that has been seasoned on top of the vegetables.

- Roast the lamb on the griddle for about 20 minutes, then turn down the heat to 325°F. Keep roasting the meat until it reaches the doneness you want, about 90 minutes for medium-rare. If you put a thermometer in the middle, it should read 130°F.
- Let the leg of lamb rest for 30 minutes on a cutting board with a tent made of aluminum foil before you cut it. Put the vegetables on a serving tray and cover them with aluminum foil until it's time to serve. This will keep the vegetables warm.

7. Classic Beef Stew

(Preparation time: 15 minutes | Cooking time: 2 hours 20 minutes | Servings: 4 | Difficulty: Medium)

Per serving: Calories 529, Total fat 18g, Protein 49g, Carbs 7g

Ingredients:

- 10 cups of meat broth
- 3 tablespoons of flour
- 1 sprig of thyme
- 36 oz. of priest's hat
- 1 carrot
- Olive oil to taste
- 1 stick of celery
- Salt & pepper to taste
- 1 white onion
- 1 sprig of rosemary
- 2 sage leaves
- 1 glass of red wine

Instructions:

- Before chopping the carrot and onion, they should be peeled and washed.
- Chop the celery after it has been washed.
- Wash and dry the thyme, sage, and rosemary.
- After washing and drying the meat, remove any excess fat and cut it into cubes.
- Inside a mixing bowl, combine the meat with the flour and whisk well.
- Preheat your griddle at medium heat.

- Place the saucepan on the griddle for about 10 minutes to preheat.
- Pour in 3 tablespoons olive oil when it's hot and wait for it to heat up.
- Cook for 5 minutes after adding the carrot, onion, and celery to the hot oil.
- After adding the meat, cook for about 10 minutes, stirring frequently.
- Allow the red wine to evaporate after it has been added.
- Season with salt and black pepper, then add the aromatic herbs and meat broth and cook on indirect heat.
- Cook for about 2 hours, stirring occasionally, with the lid on the saucepan.
- After cooking, remove the saucepan from the griddle and set it aside to cool for 5 minutes.
- Serve the meat with the cooking juices drizzled over it.

8. Rack of Beef with Potatoes and Mushrooms

(Preparation time: 20 minutes | Cooking time: 1 hour 30 minutes | Servings: 6 | Difficulty: Medium)

Per serving: Calories 651, Total fat 21g, Protein 41g, Carbs 31g

Ingredients:

- 1 glass of white wine
- 5 medium-sized potatoes
- 1 cup of porcini mushrooms
- Olive oil to taste
- 4 sage leaves
- 1 cup of pumpkin pulp
- 2 cloves of garlic
- 1 sprig of rosemary
- Salt & pepper to taste
- 42 oz. of a rack of beef with 4 ribs

Instructions:

- Wash and dry the beef rack to get rid of any excess fat.
- Before slicing the mushrooms, remove the earthy section and wash and dry them.

- Before cutting the pumpkin pulp into cubes, it should be washed and dried.
- Before cutting the potatoes into cubes, they should be peeled and washed.
- Before chopping garlic cloves, they should be peeled and washed.
- Sage and rosemary should be washed and dried before using.
- Preheat your griddle at medium-high.
- A baking pan should be sprayed with olive oil.
- Brush the rack with olive oil and season with salt and pepper before placing it in the baking pan.
- Place the baking pan with the garlic, sage, rosemary, and a splash of white wine on the griddle.
- Cook for 1 hour, flipping the meat every 20 minutes and keeping the top covered.
- Meanwhile, combine the squash, mushrooms, and potatoes in a mixing bowl.
- To combine flavors, season with oil, salt, and pepper and toss well.
- After an hour, add the vegetables to the pan.
- Cook for an additional 30 minutes.
- After the meat has finished cooking, remove it from the griddle and set it aside to rest for 10 minutes.
- Cut the meat rack into four pieces now.
- Arrange the rack pieces on the plates. Serve alongside the vegetables.

9. Texas-Style Brisket

(Preparation time: 10 minutes | Cooking time: 6 hours 20 minutes | Servings: 6 | Difficulty: Easy)

Per serving: Calories 591, Total fat 43g, Protein 46g, Carbs 3g

Ingredients:

- 1 (4 1/2 lb.) of flat-cut beef brisket (around 3 inches thick)

For the rub:

- 1 teaspoon of onion powder
- 2 teaspoons of smoked paprika
- 1 tablespoon of sea salt
- 1 teaspoon of ground black pepper
- 1 tablespoon of dark brown sugar

- 1 teaspoon of mesquite liquid smoke, like Colgin
- 2 teaspoons of chili powder
- 1 teaspoon of garlic powder

Instructions:

- Combine the rub ingredients inside a small-sized mixing bowl.
- Before applying the coffee mixture, rinse and pat dry the brisket.
- Preheat your griddle for two-zone cooking, one on high and one on low.
- Spray the griddle top using cooking spray.
- Sear for 3 to 5 minutes per side on high heat or until beautifully charred.
- Cook for 6 hours on low, tenting with foil, till a meat thermometer registers 195°F.
- Take them off the griddle. Allow 30 minutes of covered standing time.
- Brisket should be thinly sliced across the grain. Serve and have fun!

10. Double-Cut Grilled Pork Chop with Sweet & Sour Peaches

(Preparation time: 20 minutes | Cooking time: 1-hour | Servings: 4 | Difficulty: Easy)

Per serving: Calories 519, Total fat 26g, Protein 58g, Carbs 9g

Ingredients:

- 4 large double-cut pork chops
- 1/2 cup of Madeira
- 1 teaspoon of black pepper
- 1 1/2 cups of high west whiskey
- 2 whole scallions
- 1 cup of orange juice
- 2 sliced whole onions
- 3 tablespoons of Pork & Poultry Rub
- 4 whole peaches, halved
- 3/4 cup of sherry vinegar
- 2 tablespoons of olive oil
- 1/2 cup of honey

Instructions:

- Preheat your griddle at medium-high heat.
- Bring the whiskey, orange juice, honey, sherry, Madeira, and black pepper to a boiling in a pan on the griddle for the Whiskey Reduction. Cook for about an hour or till the sauce thickens and becomes syrupy. Reserve.
- Preheat a pan on the griddle for the peaches. Incorporate the extra virgin olive oil. In a pan, place the onion slices, peaches, and sliced scallions, cut side down. Cook for about 20 minutes, or till the peaches and onions are caramelized, and the scallions are softening, rotating the onions and scallions as needed. When ready to serve, set aside and reheat.
- Pork Chops: Thoroughly season pork chops with Pork & Poultry Rub. Cook for about 25 minutes on each side of the griddle or till the internal temperature reaches around 140°F. Remove from the griddle and set it aside for 5 minutes before slicing.
- Drizzle the whiskey reduction over the pork chops, onions, peaches, and scallions just before serving.

11. Pork Skewers with Avocado and Cherry Tomatoes

(Preparation time: 10 minutes | Cooking time: 10 minutes | Servings: 4 | Difficulty: Medium)

Per serving: Calories 295, Total fat 18g, Protein 36g, Carbs 8g

Ingredients:

- 2 tablespoons of apple cider vinegar
- 8 cherry tomatoes
- 2 teaspoons of honey
- 1 avocado
- 14 oz. of pork loin
- Olive oil to taste
- 2 tablespoons of mustard
- 1 teaspoon of chopped chives
- Salt & pepper to taste

Instructions:

- To begin, peel the avocado, leaving only the pulp behind. After removing the central core, cut it into cubes.
- Cut the cherry tomatoes in half after washing them.
- Before cutting the loin into cubes the same length as the avocado, it should be washed and dried.
- To make the skewers, alternately insert the pork cubes, half a tomato, and avocado cubes onto the steel skewers.
- In the meantime, make the marinade.
- Inside a large-sized mixing bowl, combine the mustard, vinegar, salt, honey, oil, chives, and pepper.
- Place the skewers in the dish, cover them with plastic wrap, and set aside for an hour to marinate.
- After an hour, take the skewers out of the fridge.
- Preheat the griddle at medium heat.
- Spray the griddle top using cooking spray.
- Place the skewers on the griddle and cook for 8 minutes, flipping halfway through.
- As soon as they're done, take them off the griddle, place them on plates, and serve immediately with the marinating juice.

12. Lamb with Mint Orange Sauce

(Preparation time: 15 minutes | Cooking time: 20 minutes | Servings: 5 | Difficulty: Medium)

Per serving: Calories 438, Total fat 30g, Protein 27g, Carbs 12g

Ingredients:

- 2 tablespoons of olive oil
- 1 tablespoon of cumin
- ½ teaspoon of ground coriander
- 1 pinch of cayenne pepper
- 2 pounds of lamb loin chops
- Salt as needed
- ½ teaspoon of black pepper

- 3 cloves of garlic, minced
- ¼ teaspoon of cinnamon
- 1 teaspoon of mixed herbs - Italian, Greek, or French blend

For the sauce:

- 1 tablespoon of chopped fresh mint
- ½ tablespoon of rice vinegar
- 1 pinch of hot chili flakes
- ¼ cup of orange marmalade

Instructions:

- Inside a large-sized mixing bowl, combine the lamb chops. Seasonings include olive oil, garlic, cumin, coriander, mixed herbs, pepper, cayenne pepper, cinnamon, and salt. Toss everything till the oil and seasonings are evenly distributed. After wrapping in plastic wrap, place in the refrigerator. Allow for at least 4 hours of marinating time.

- Preheat your griddle at medium-high heat and coat it with a thin layer of oil. Cook the chops on the griddle. Season the chops with salt and black pepper. Cook for 4 to 7 minutes on the first side, depending on the size of the chops. Before flipping the chops, give them a half-turn on the griddle for about a minute. Cook for another 4 to 7 minutes on the opposite side or till done to preference. An instant-read thermometer placed in the center should read 125 to 130°F for medium-rare. Cover loosely with foil and transfer to a serving dish.

- Put the marmalade in a bowl. Combine the mint, chili flakes, and rice vinegar inside a mixing bowl.

- Before serving, brush the sauce over the chops.

13. Lamb Loaf

(Preparation time: 15 minutes | Cooking time: 35 minutes | Servings: 4 | Difficulty: Easy)

Per serving: Calories 409, Total fat 30g, Protein 22g, Carbs 12g

Ingredients:

- 1 pound of ground lamb
- 5 finely chopped leaves, fresh mint
- 1 teaspoon of dried basil
- ½ teaspoon of vegetable oil
- 2 slices of dry bread, diced

- ¼ teaspoon of ground black pepper
- 1 teaspoon of ground coriander
- 1 egg
- 2 tablespoons of chopped fresh thyme
- ½ teaspoon of vegetable oil, or as required
- 1 tablespoon of lemon zest
- ¼ cup of milk
- 1 teaspoon of crushed dried rosemary
- ¾ teaspoon of salt
- 1 tablespoon of Worcestershire sauce
- 2 tablespoons of balsamic vinegar
- ¼ cup of tomato sauce
- 4 cloves of minced garlic

Instructions:

- Preheat your griddle at medium heat. Grease a 9x5-inch loaf pan lightly.
- Inside a small-sized mixing bowl, combine the milk and bread. To absorb the milk, press the bread with a fork.
- Inside a medium-sized mixing bowl, combine the lamb, egg, garlic, thyme, coriander, Worcestershire sauce, lemon zest, salt, basil, rosemary, and pepper. Stir in the soaked bread and any remaining milk. Using your hands, combine everything till it's completely smooth. Place the meatloaf in the greased pan.
- Evenly distribute the tomato sauce and mint on the meatloaf. Pour the balsamic vinegar on top. Place the pan on the griddle.
- Cook for around 35 minutes or till the center is no longer pink. In the center, an instant-read thermometer should read at least 160°F. Remove from the griddle and set aside for 5 minutes to cool before serving.

14. Moroccan-Spiced Rack of Lamb

(Preparation time: 15 minutes | Cooking time: 25 minutes | Servings: 4 | Difficulty: Easy)

Per serving: Calories 413, Total fat 34g, Protein 22g, Carbs 2g

Ingredients:

- 1 (8 bones) rack Lamb, domestic, rib, separable lean & fat, trimmed to 1/8" fat, choice, raw

- ¼ cup of chopped fresh mint
- 2 tablespoons of olive oil
- ½ teaspoon of ground black pepper
- 1 pinch of ground cloves, or to taste
- ½ teaspoon ground coriander
- 2 tablespoons of chopped fresh parsley
- 1 ½ teaspoons of ground ginger
- ½ teaspoon of ground cinnamon
- ½ teaspoon of ground allspice
- ½ teaspoon of ground paprika
- 1 pinch of cayenne pepper, or to taste
- ½ teaspoon of salt

Instructions:

- Inside a small-sized bowl, combine the mint, ginger, olive oil, parsley, pepper, allspice, cinnamon, cayenne, paprika, coriander, salt, and cloves to make a paste.
- Place the rack in a large glass or ceramic dish and coat it with the herb paste. Marinate in the refrigerator for 30 to 60 minutes, covered with plastic wrap.
- Preheat your griddle at medium heat and coat it using a thin layer of oil.
- Remove the rack from the fridge and place it on the griddle, meat side up.
- Cook for around 20 to 25 minutes on the griddle or till an instant-read thermometer inserted in the center reads 125°F for rare or 130°F for medium-rare.
- Remove it from the griddle and cover it loosely using foil. After each set, allow for a 5- to the 10-minute recovery period.
- Carve the meat to serve by cutting between the ribs.

15. Beef Chili

(Preparation time: 15 minutes | Cooking time: 2 hours | Servings: 4 | Difficulty: Medium)

Per serving: Calories 476, Total fat 15g, Protein 47g, Carbs 13g

Ingredients:

- 2 cups of tomato puree
- 1 tablespoon of brown sugar
- 28 oz. of ground beef
- 1 tablespoon of cumin powder
- 3 cups of pre-cooked black beans
- 1 cup of red peppers
- 3 cloves of garlic
- Salt & pepper to taste
- 1 red onion
- 1 chopped chili
- Olive oil to taste
- 1 white onion
- 2 cups of meat broth
- 1 tablespoon of coriander powder

Instructions:

- Garlic cloves and red and white onions should be peeled and washed before being finely chopped.
- Remove the pepper's cap, seeds, and white pepper filaments. It should be washed before being cut into cubes.
- Preheat your griddle at medium heat.
- Preheat the cast-iron saucepan for about 10 minutes on the griddle.
- As soon as the pan is hot, add 2 tablespoons of olive oil.
- Now add the meat, mix it in, and brown it for a few minutes.
- After adding the garlic and onion, cook for another 2 minutes.

- Cook for 5 minutes more after adding the pepper, chili, salt, brown sugar, coriander, cumin, and pepper.
- After that, toss in the tomato after adding the beef broth.
- Cook for about 60 minutes, stirring occasionally, with the lid on the saucepan.
- After 60 minutes, add the beans and the preservation liquid and cook for another 40 minutes, covered.
- After cooking, remove the saucepan from the griddle and set it aside to cool for about 10 minutes.
- Serve the beef chili immediately on serving plates.

16. Tuscan-Style Steak with Crispy Potatoes

(Preparation time: 20 minutes | Cooking time: 35 minutes | Servings: 4 | Difficulty: Medium)

Per serving: Calories 366, Total fat 23g, Protein 14g, Carbs 27g

Ingredients:

- 2 teaspoons of red wine, like Sangiovese or Montepulciano
- 4 tablespoons of extra-virgin olive oil, divided
- 1 teaspoon of balsamic vinegar
- Sea salt & freshly ground pepper, to taste
- 2 bone-in porterhouse steaks
- 1 1/2 lb. of small potatoes, like Yukon Gold, scrubbed but skins left on, halved
- 3 fresh rosemary sprigs, needles removed (discard stems)
- Pinch red pepper flakes

Instructions:

- Fill a large-sized pot halfway with water and add the potatoes. Bring to the boil over a high flame, then reduce to medium flame and cook for 10 minutes or till the potatoes are almost soft. Drain, then transfer to a medium-sized mixing bowl and drizzle with 2 tablespoons olive oil.
- Preheat your griddle at medium-high heat and coat it using a thin layer of oil.
- Inside a mixing bowl, combine vinegar, 2 tablespoons of olive oil, red wine, rosemary, and pepper flakes; add the steaks and marinate till ready to cook.
- Season the potatoes with salt & pepper.
- Place the steaks on one side of the griddle and the potatoes on the other.

- Cook the steak for 5 minutes on one side for medium-rare, then flip and cook for another 4 minutes.
- After adding the potatoes, cook for about 5 minutes.
- While the potatoes are cooking, place the steaks on a cutting board and tent with aluminum foil for 5 minutes to rest.
- Cut each steak into two pieces and serve on four dinner plates. Serve immediately with sprinkled potatoes around the steak.

17. Pork Skewers with Apple and Feta

(Preparation time: 15 minutes | Cooking time: 15 minutes | Servings: 4 | Difficulty: Medium)

Per serving: Calories 237, Total fat 15g, Protein 24g, Carbs 7g

Ingredients:

- 7 oz. of diced feta
- 2 tablespoons of mayonnaise
- 1 teaspoon of chopped chives
- 10 oz. of pork loin
- 2 teaspoons of maple syrup
- 1 red apple
- Salt & pepper to taste
- 2 tablespoons of balsamic vinegar
- Olive oil to taste

Instructions:

- Before cutting the meat into pieces, wash and dry it.
- The apple should be peeled and washed as well.
- Remove the inner seeds, split them in half, and cut them into cubes roughly the size of the meat.
- Assemble the skewers by alternating the meat, feta, and apple cubes.
- In the meantime, prepare the marinade for the skewers.
- Inside a large mixing bowl, combine the mayonnaise, vinegar, salt, maple syrup, oil, chives, and pepper.

- Place the skewers in the dish, cover using plastic wrap, and set them aside for an hour to marinate.
- Preheat your griddle at medium heat.
- Spray the griddle top using cooking spray.
- After marinating, drain the skewers and place them on the griddle.
- Cook for approximately 8 minutes, flipping the skewers on all sides.
- As soon as they're done, remove them from the griddle, place them on plates, and serve immediately.

18. Pork Chops Stuffed with Cheese

(Preparation time: 20 minutes | Cooking time: 15 minutes | Servings: 4 | Difficulty: Medium)

Per serving: Calories 547, Total fat 29g, Protein 51g, Carbs 3g

Ingredients:

- 2 tablespoons of cognac
- 1 clove of garlic
- ½ glass of white wine
- 4 pork chops (7 oz. each)
- Olive oil to taste
- 1 teaspoon of chopped juniper berries
- 5 oz. of provolone
- 1 sprig of rosemary

Instructions:

- Before chopping garlic, it should be peeled and washed.
- After washing and drying the rosemary, cut the needles into small pieces.
- Wash and dry the pork chops to remove all of the excess fat.
- Make a horizontal slit in the chops and insert the garlic and rosemary.
- Sliced provolone cheese should be inserted into the meat.
- Secure and hold the chops in place using kitchen twine.
- To make a homogeneous emulsion, combine pepper, 4 tablespoons olive oil, salt, white wine, juniper berries, and cognac in a mixing bowl.

- Brush the emulsion on both sides of the chops.
- Preheat the griddle at medium heat and spray the griddle top using cooking spray.
- Cook the chops for about 5 minutes per side on the griddle, turning frequently and brushing using the emulsion.
- When the chops are done, remove them from the griddle and set them aside to rest for a few minutes.
- Before serving, remove the kitchen string from the chops.

19. Habanero-Marinated Pork Chops

(Preparation time: 20 minutes | Cooking time: 15 minutes | Servings: 4 | Difficulty: Easy)
Per serving: Calories 490, Total fat 39g, Protein 23g, Carbs 11g
Ingredients:

- 3 tablespoons of olive oil, plus more for grill
- Kosher salt & freshly ground black pepper
- 4 ½-inch-thick bone-in pork chops

For the marinade:

- 2 garlic cloves, minced
- ½ cup of fresh orange juice
- 1 tablespoon of apple cider vinegar
- 2 tablespoons of brown sugar
- 1 habanero chili, seeded, chopped fine

Instructions:

- Combine the marinade ingredients inside a large-sized sealable plastic bag.
- Before placing the pork chops in the bag, pierce them all over with a fork, seal them, and turn to coat.
- Marinate at room temperature for 30 minutes, turning occasionally.
- Preheat the griddle over medium-high heat.
- Coat the griddle in oil with a brush.
- Remove the pork chops from the marinade and pat them dry.
- Sear for 8 minutes or till blackened and cooked through, turning occasionally.
- Place on a plate and set aside for 5 minutes to cool.
- Serve with your favorite side dish.

20. Lamb Chops in Soy Sauce

(Preparation time: 10 minutes | Cooking time: 15 minutes | Servings: 4 | Difficulty: Medium)

Per serving: Calories 320, Total fat 26g, Protein 19g, Carbs 2g

Ingredients:

- 2 tablespoons of soy sauce
- 4 lamb chops (around 5-oz./142 g)
- ¼ cup of onion, chopped roughly
- 2 chopped roughly garlic cloves
- ½ cup of extra-virgin olive oil, divided
- 1 tablespoon of chopped fresh rosemary
- Salt, to taste

- 2 tablespoons of balsamic vinegar
- 1 teaspoon of Worcestershire sauce
- Freshly ground black pepper, to taste
- 2 teaspoons of Dijon mustard

Instructions:

- Preheat your griddle at medium heat.
- Heat one tablespoon of olive oil on the griddle inside a small-sized pan and sauté the onions and garlic for about 4-5 minutes.
- Take them off the griddle and whisk together till smooth.
- Blend the vinegar, soy sauce, mustard, Worcestershire sauce, rosemary, and black pepper in a blender till smooth.
- While the machine is running, drizzle in the remaining oil slowly and pulse till smooth.
- Add the sauce to the pan on the griddle and cook for a few minutes.
- Remove the sauce from the griddle and place it in a mixing bowl to cool.
- Apply a thin layer of oil to the griddle's surface.
- Season the lamb chops evenly with salt and black pepper after coating them with the remaining oil.
- On the griddle, cook the chops for 4-6 minutes on each side.
- Remove the chops from the griddle and immediately serve with the sauce.

21. Lamb Lollipops with Yuzu Aioli

(Preparation time: 15 minutes | Cooking time: 20 minutes | Servings: 6 | Difficulty: Easy)

Per serving: Calories 990, Total fat 92g, Protein 38g, Carbs 2g

Ingredients:

- 2 frenched racks of lamb
- 1/2 cup of wild game rub

For the Yuzu Aioli:

- ¼ cup of yuzu juice, or more to taste
- 1 ½ cups of canola oil
- ½ teaspoon of white vinegar

- 1 teaspoon of Dijon mustard
- Salt to taste
- ½ lemon, juiced
- 2 eggs
- ½ cup olive oil

Instructions:

- Set aside the two lamb racks that have been chopped into 1-inch bone chops.
- Inside a metal mixing bowl, combine white vinegar, lemon juice, mustard, and salt. One at a time, whisk in the eggs.
- In a mixing bowl, combine the canola and olive oils. Slowly drizzle the blended oil into the egg mixture, whisking constantly, till it thickens and doubles in volume, resembling mayonnaise. Season using salt to taste. To achieve the desired flavor, add yuzu juice at the end.
- Preheat your griddle at medium heat and coat it using a thin layer of oil.
- Season both sides of the lamb chops with the game rub on a cutting board.
- Place the chops on the griddle that has been preheated. Cook for about 5 minutes per side for medium-rare.
- Remove them from the griddle, place them on a plate, and top them with yuzu aioli.

22. Grilled Southwestern Lamb

(Preparation time: 10 minutes | Cooking time: 25 minutes | Servings: 2 | Difficulty: Easy)

Per serving: Calories 27, Total fat 12g, Protein 33g, Carbs 11g

Ingredients:

- 1/4 cup molasses
- 2 teaspoons of sugar
- 1/2 cup of chopped onion
- 2 garlic of cloves, minced
- 1 cup of salsa
- 1/4 cup of fresh lime juice (around 2 limes)
- 1 to 3 tablespoons of chopped seeded jalapeno peppers
- 1/4 cup of chicken broth

- 4 lamb chops (around one inch thick)
- Sour cream

Instructions:

- Preheat your griddle at medium heat.
- Combine the first 8 ingredients in a griddle-safe saucepan. Cook for about 15-20 minutes, uncovered.
- Apply a thin layer of oil to the griddle.
- Cook lamb chops on the griddle for 10-15 minutes for medium-rare and 15 to 20 minutes for medium, flipping once. During the last few minutes of cooking, brush with sauce.
- Serve with the sour cream.

23. Sliced Beef with Asparagus and Honey Sauce

(Preparation time: 20 minutes | Cooking time: 20 minutes | Servings: 4 | Difficulty: Medium)

Per serving: Calories 189, Total fat 12g, Protein 23g, Carbs 9g

Ingredients:

- 3 tablespoons of sesame seed oil
- 14 oz. of beef tenderloin
- 3 tablespoons of red wine vinegar
- Salt & pepper to taste
- 12 green asparagus
- Olive oil to taste
- 4 tablespoons of honey

Instructions:

- Remove the stalk and the toughest part of the asparagus. They should be washed, dried, and boiled for 5 minutes in salted water.
- Drain and rinse them underneath cold water after they've been cooked.
- After washing and drying the meat, remove any excess fat.
- After brushing the meat with olive oil, season it using salt and pepper.
- Preheat your griddle at medium-high heat.
- Cook the meat for about 5 minutes per side on the griddle, or till the internal temperature reaches 131°F.
- Remove the meat from the griddle and set it aside for 10 minutes to rest.
- Cook the asparagus for a few minutes on the griddle.
- Remove the asparagus from the griddle and divide it among the serving dishes.
- Combine the honey, sesame oil, a tablespoon of olive oil, and the vinegar inside a mixing bowl.
- Stir the emulsion till it is completely homogeneous.
- Serve the steak in slices with the asparagus on plates.
- Garnish with a dollop of honey sauce.

24. Beef Meatballs in Sweet and Sour Sauce

(Preparation time: 20 minutes | Cooking time: 30 minutes | Servings: 6 | Difficulty: Medium)

Per serving: Calories 510, Total fat 14g, Protein 35g, Carbs 32g

Ingredients:

- 1/2 cup of brown sugar
- 2 tablespoons of milk
- 1 glass of balsamic vinegar
- 1/2 cup of breadcrumbs
- 21 oz. of minced beef
- Olive oil to taste
- 1/2 cup of grated Parmesan cheese
- Salt & pepper to taste

- 1 sprig of chopped parsley
- 2 eggs

Instructions:

- Combine the beef, breadcrumbs, milk, Parmesan, pepper, parsley, milk, salt, and eggs inside a mixing bowl.
- Stir till the mixture is moist and homogeneous.
- Make spherical meatballs that aren't too big.
- Preheat your griddle at medium heat.
- Place a plate on a heated griddle that has been brushed with olive oil for 10 minutes.
- Place the meatballs on the plate and cook for about 20 minutes, rotating frequently, with the lid closed.
- After the meatballs have finished cooking, remove them from the griddle and heat the wok on the griddle.
- Stir in the sugar and vinegar till the sugar has completely melted and caramelized.
- Remove the wok from the griddle and add the meatballs.
- Stir to combine the flavors of the meatballs and the sauce.
- Place the meatballs on plates now. Serve with the wok sauce that was left over.

25. Goulash

(Preparation time: 20 minutes | Cooking time: 3 hours | Servings: 6 | Difficulty: Medium)

Per serving: Calories 327, Total fat 12g, Protein 26g, Carbs 9g

Ingredients:

- 4 cups of meat broth
- 36 oz. of sirloin steak
- 1 cup of tomato pulp
- 2 bay leaves
- 1 lemon
- Salt & pepper to taste
- 2 onions
- 1 tablespoon of cumin

- Olive oil to taste
- 2 tablespoons of vinegar
- 1 clove of garlic
- 2 teaspoons of paprika

Instructions:

- Bay leaves should be washed and dried before use.
- Before chopping the onions and garlic cloves, they should be peeled and washed.
- After the lemon has been washed and dried, grate the zest.
- After washing and drying the sirloin steak, trim the excess fat and cut it into cubes.
- Preheat your griddle at medium heat.
- Put the saucepan on the griddle and let it heat for around 10 minutes.
- Add 2 tablespoons of olive oil and when it is hot enough, brown the onion and garlic in it.
- Before adding the paprika, let the vinegar evaporate.
- Now add the meat, cumin, bay leaf, salt, lemon zest, tomato pulp, and pepper.
- Cook for about 5 minutes after thoroughly mixing.
- Pour in the broth, and cover the saucepan.
- Cook, stirring occasionally, for about 2 hours and 30 minutes.
- After it has finished cooking, remove it from the griddle and remove the bay leaves.
- Drizzle the cooking liquids over the Goulash in serving bowls.

Chapter 10: Game Meat Recipes

1. Smothered Pheasant

(Preparation time: 10 minutes | Cooking time: 1 hour 45 minutes | Servings: 6 | Difficulty: Easy)

Per serving: Calories 521, Total fat 31g, Protein 48g, Carbs 11g

Ingredients:

- ½ cup of all-purpose flour
- 6 skinless and boneless pheasant breast halves
- 2 cups of half-and-half cream
- Salt and black pepper to taste
- ½ cup of butter

Instructions:

- Preheat your griddle at medium heat and spray the griddle top using cooking spray.
- Season pheasant breasts using salt and pepper on all sides. On a plate, sprinkle the flour and push the pheasant breast into it till completely coated. Remove any excess flour & set aside. Melt the butter inside a deep skillet or ovenproof Dutch oven on the griddle. Cook pheasant breasts inside the hot butter for 5 minutes per side or till golden brown on both sides. Bring the half-and-half cream to a simmer and cover the Dutch oven.
- Cook for around 1 1/2 hours or till the pheasant breasts are soft and no longer pink in the center. In the center, an instant-read thermometer must read at least 165 degrees F.

2. Pheasant Poppers

(Preparation time: 10 minutes | Cooking time: 15 minutes | Servings: 6 | Difficulty: Easy)

Per serving: Calories 310, Total fat 18g, Protein 33g, Carbs 2g

Ingredients:

- 1 (4 ounces) jar of sliced jalapeno peppers
- 6 bamboo skewers, soaked inside water for around 20 minutes
- 1 ½ pounds of pheasant breast
- 36 toothpicks
- 12 slices of bacon, sliced into thirds

Instructions:

- Place the pheasant breast inside a bowl and cut it into 36 pieces. Pour the jalapeno pepper liquid over the pheasant, mix, and set aside for 20 minutes to marinate.
- Preheat your griddle at medium heat and spray the griddle top using cooking spray.
- Remove the pheasant from the marinade and set it aside. Wrap each pheasant breast with 1/3 of a strip of bacon and a slice of jalapeno pepper. Skewer 6 pieces of pheasant on each skewer.
- Cook, turning frequently, on a preheated griddle till the bacon is crispy, around 15 to 20 minutes. To serve, remove the skewers out of the pheasant pieces and insert a toothpick into each piece.

3. Breaded Pheasant Nuggets

(Preparation time: 10 minutes | Cooking time: 50 minutes | Servings: 4 | Difficulty: Easy)

Per serving: Calories 607, Total fat 58g, Protein 56g, Carbs 28g

Ingredients:

- ½ teaspoon of dry mustard powder
- 2 ½ cups of Italian-style panko bread crumbs
- ¾ cup of butter
- 1 tablespoon of dried parsley
- ½ teaspoon of ground black pepper
- 2 cloves of minced garlic
- ½ cup of grated Parmesan cheese
- 6 skinless and boneless pheasant breast halves, sliced into chunks

- 2 teaspoons of salt

Instructions:

- Preheat your griddle at medium heat and spray the griddle top using cooking spray.

- Inside a mixing bowl, combine the panko, black pepper, salt, Parmesan cheese, parsley, and mustard powder until evenly combined.

- Inside a skillet on the griddle, melt the butter with garlic. Cook and mix the garlic for around 5 minutes after it has melted to flavor the butter. Once melted, pour into mixing bowl. Dip the pheasant into melted butter, then into the panko crumbs. Place in a single layer on an ungreased baking sheet. Sprinkle the pheasant nuggets with the remaining panko crumbs.

- Cook for around 45 minutes on the griddle or till the pheasant chunks is no longer pink in the center.

4. Deer Poppers

(Preparation time: 10 minutes | Cooking time: 30 minutes | Servings: 10 | Difficulty: Easy)

Per serving: Calories 308, Total fat 26g, Protein 13g, Carbs 5g

Ingredients:

- 1 (16-ounces) bottle of Italian salad dressing
- Toothpicks soaked in water
- 1 pound of cubed venison steaks
- ½ teaspoon of Greek seasoning, or to taste
- 10 slices of bacon, sliced in half
- ¼ teaspoon of steak seasoning, or to taste
- ½ cup of jalapeno pepper slices

Instructions:

- Season the venison with Greek seasoning as well as steak seasoning.

- Pour enough Italian dressing into a bowl to cover. Refrigerate for at least 2 hours, preferably overnight, to marinate.

- Preheat the griddle at medium heat and coat the griddle top using cooking spray. Remove the meat from the marinade and set aside. Wrap a slice of bacon around a piece of meat and a slice of jalapeno. Use a soaked toothpick to secure. Rep with the remaining meat.

- Cook the deer poppers for around 15 to 20 minutes, turning halfway through to brown the bacon. Serve and have fun!

5. Drunk Deer Chili

(Preparation time: 10 minutes | Cooking time: 1 hour 15 minutes | Servings: 10 | Difficulty: Easy)

Per serving: Calories 403, Total fat 22g, Protein 30g, Carbs 14g

Ingredients:

- 1 large chopped onion
- ¼ cup of butter
- 4 cubes of crumbled beef bouillon
- 1 pound of ground venison
- 1 pound of cubed pork stew meat
- 3 tablespoons of chili powder
- 1 pound of cubed beef stew meat
- ½ teaspoon of cayenne pepper
- 1 fresh seeded and minced jalapeno pepper
- 2 (14 ounces) cans of stewed tomatoes, with the juice
- 1 ½ teaspoons of ground cumin
- 2 cups of water
- 1 (15-ounce) can of tomato sauce
- 2 (12 fluid ounces) cans of pilsner-style beer
- 6 minced cloves of garlic
- ¼ cup of Kentucky bourbon

Instructions:

- Preheat the griddle at medium heat.
- Inside a large-sized pot on the griddle, melt the butter. Brown the beef, venison, and pork inside melted butter.
- Cook till the onion and jalapeno are tender. Add the cayenne pepper, chili powder, and cumin and mix well.
- Combine the stewed tomatoes, garlic, tomato sauce, and beef bouillon. Pour in the beer, bourbon, and water and stir well. Bring the chili up to the boil.
- Reduce the griddle heat to medium-low, cover, and simmer for around 1 hour, stirring frequently.

6. Buffalo Meatloaf

(Preparation time: 10 minutes | Cooking time: 1 hour 30 minutes | Servings: 4 | Difficulty: Easy)

Per serving: Calories 179, Total fat 4g, Protein 24g, Carbs 13g

Ingredients:

- 1 teaspoon of mustard powder
- 1 slice of multigrain bread
- 1 diced onion
- ⅓ cup of ketchup
- 1 pound of ground buffalo meat
- ¾ cup of canned diced tomatoes, drained
- 1 lightly beaten egg
- 1 dash of ground black pepper
- 1 teaspoon of salt

Instructions:

- Preheat the griddle at medium heat.
- Set aside the bread slice that has been crumbled into crumbs. Grease an 8x8 baking dish using cooking spray.

- Inside a large-sized mixing bowl, thoroughly combine pepper, ground buffalo meat, salt, onion, egg, tomatoes, ground mustard, and bread crumbs.

- Shape the meat mixture into an 8x4-inch loaf and place it in the center of the baking dish. Cover the top and edges of the meatloaf using ketchup.

- Put the pan on the griddle and cook for around 1 1/2 hours, till the meat is no longer pink and the ketchup forms a coating over the meatloaf. Allow standing for around 10 minutes prior to serving.

7. Colorado Buffalo Chili

(Preparation time: 10 minutes | Cooking time: 8 hours 10 minutes | Servings: 6 | Difficulty: Medium)

Per serving: Calories 219, Total fat 3g, Protein 22g, Carbs 30g

Ingredients:

- 1 (14.5 ounces) can of drained kidney beans
- 1-pound of ground buffalo
- 1 teaspoon of red pepper flakes
- ½ teaspoon of ground cumin
- 1 (10-ounces) can of diced tomatoes with the green chiles
- 1 chopped Anaheim chile pepper
- 1 pinch of cayenne pepper, or to taste
- ½ medium chopped onion
- 1 (10.75 ounces) can of tomato soup
- Salt & ground black pepper to taste
- 1 (15-ounce) can of drained chili beans
- 2 tablespoons of chili powder
- ½ teaspoon of minced garlic
- 1 chopped poblano chile pepper
- ½ teaspoon of cayenne pepper
- 1 ½ teaspoons of ground cumin

Instructions:

- Preheat the griddle at medium heat.

- Place the skillet on the griddle.
- Inside a skillet on the griddle, brown the buffalo; season using 1/2 teaspoon of cumin and 1 pinch of cayenne pepper to taste. Excess grease should be drained.
- Turn the griddle at low heat.
- Inside a slow cooker, mix together the onion, buffalo, red pepper flakes, tomatoes with green chiles, chili powder, tomato soup, chili beans, garlic, Anaheim chile pepper, kidney beans, poblano chile pepper, 1 1/2 teaspoons of cumin, 1/2 teaspoon of cayenne pepper, black pepper and salt. Cook for around 8 hours.

8. Deer Jerky

(Preparation time: 15 minutes | Cooking time: 6 hours 10 minutes | Servings: 8 | Difficulty: Easy)

Per serving: Calories 111, Total fat 5g, Protein 14g, Carbs 3g

Ingredients:

- 1 pound of boneless venison roast
- 4 tablespoons of soy sauce
- ¼ teaspoon of pepper
- 1 tablespoon of ketchup
- 4 tablespoons of Worcestershire sauce
- ½ teaspoon of salt
- ¼ teaspoon of garlic powder
- 2 tablespoons of liquid smoke flavoring
- ¼ teaspoon of onion salt

Instructions:

- Inside a large-sized resealable plastic bag, combine garlic powder, soy sauce, liquid smoke, Worcestershire sauce, pepper, ketchup, salt, and onion salt; set aside.
- Venison should be cut into 1-inch wide by 1/8-inch thick strips. Seal the bag after adding the strips to the marinade. Refrigerate for 8 to 12 hours, occasionally kneading to distribute marinade evenly.

- Preheat the griddle at medium heat and place a pan on the griddle.
- Shake off any excess marinade from the venison.
- Place venison in a single layer on a baking pan in the griddle and dehydrate in a griddle for 6 to 8 hours, or till desired texture is achieved.

9. Blue Stuffed Buffalo Burger

(Preparation time: 10 minutes | Cooking time: 15 minutes | Servings: 8 | Difficulty: Easy)

Per serving: Calories 686, Total fat 25g, Protein 39g, Carbs 38g

Ingredients:

- ½ cup of mayonnaise
- 2 pounds of ground buffalo
- 8 slices of tomato
- ½ cup of crumbled blue cheese
- 2 teaspoons of salt
- 8 leaves Bibb lettuce
- Ground black pepper to taste
- 8 whole wheat hamburger buns, split & toasted
- ½ red onion, cut into half-inch slices

Instructions:

- Preheat the griddle at medium heat and coat the griddle top using cooking spray.
- Season ground buffalo using salt and pepper and shape it into eight balls. With your thumb, press a cavity halfway through each ball; insert a tablespoon of the blue cheese into hole and lock the meat around cheese. Shape each ball into a patty.
- Cook the burgers on the griddle till done to your liking, 4 to 6 minutes on each side for well done. In the center, an instant-read thermometer should read 160 degrees F. Spread mayonnaise on the toasted buns. Place a burger patty on the bottom of each bun, then top with onion rings, lettuce leaf, and tomato slices. To serve, top with remaining buns.

10. Tender Pheasants

(Preparation time: 10 minutes | Cooking time: 5 hours 15 minutes | Servings: 8 | Difficulty: Easy)

Per serving: Calories 256, Total fat 18g, Protein 20g, Carbs 4g

Ingredients:

- 1 cup of sour cream
- 4 small pheasants, cleaned & rinsed
- 1 (10.75 ounces) can of condensed cream of mushroom soup
- 1 cup of water
- Salt & ground black pepper to taste
- 1 chopped small onion
- 1 (1 ounce) package of dry onion soup mix
- ½ pound of sliced bacon
- 1 (4.5 ounces) can of sliced mushrooms

Instructions:

- Preheat the griddle at medium heat.
- The pheasants should be put inside a large-sized slow cooker on the griddle. Wrap the bacon around the pheasants and drape it over them as much as you can. Inside a mixing bowl, whisk together the condensed soup, sour cream, water, chopped onion, onion soup mix, and mushrooms. Salt and pepper can be added to taste. Put on top of the pheasants.
- Cook for around 8 to 10 hours on Low or 5 to 7 hours on High.

11. Venison Fajitas

(Preparation time: 10 minutes | Cooking time: 20 minutes | Servings: 6 | Difficulty: Easy)

Per serving: Calories 688, Total fat 23g, Protein 39g, Carbs 38g

Ingredients:

- 1 medium-sized yellow bell pepper, cut into two-inch strips
- 2 teaspoons of seasoned salt
- ¼ teaspoon of garlic salt
- 1 medium-sized red bell pepper, cut into two-inch strips
- ½ teaspoon of black pepper
- 1 teaspoon of dried oregano
- 4 tablespoons of vegetable oil
- 1 medium onion, cut into half-inch wedges

- ½ teaspoon of cayenne pepper
- 12 warmed fajita-size flour tortillas
- 1 ½ pounds of venison, cut into two-inch strips

Instructions:

- To make the fajita seasoning, mix together seasoned salt, cayenne pepper, black pepper, garlic salt, and oregano. Spread two teaspoons of seasoning all over the sliced venison. Mix well, put the lid on, and chill for 30 minutes.
- Preheat the griddle at medium heat and coat the griddle top using cooking spray.
- Bell peppers and onions should be cooked on the griddle till they start to soften, then taken out. Pour in the rest of the oil and cook the venison on the griddle till it turns brown. Put the pepper mixture back in the pan, add the rest of the fajita seasoning, and heat it up. Serve with warmed tortillas.

12. Venison Stew

(Preparation time: 20 minutes | Cooking time: 2 hours 10 minutes | Servings: 6 | Difficulty: Easy)

Per serving: Calories 429, Total fat 9g, Protein 40g, Carbs 47g

Ingredients:

- 3 medium onions, chopped
- 1 tablespoon of Worcestershire sauce
- ½ teaspoon of dried oregano
- 2 tablespoons of vegetable oil
- ¼ cup of all-purpose flour
- 2 pounds of venison stew meat
- 1 pound of carrots, cut into one-inch pieces
- 2 minced cloves of garlic
- 3 cups of water
- 7 peeled and quartered small potatoes
- 1 tablespoon of salt
- ¼ cup of water
- 1 large bay leaf

Instructions:

- Preheat the griddle at medium heat.
- On the griddle, warm the oil inside a large-sized, heavy saucepan. When the venison has reached an even brown color, after 5 to 7 minutes of cooking and stirring, remove it from the pan. During the next 5 minutes, add the onions and garlic and cook while stirring till the onions become translucent. Add the water, oregano, Worcestershire, salt, and bay leaf, and mix well. For the next two hours or so, with the lid on, the venison should be nice and tender.
- Add carrots and potatoes, mixing well; cook for around 15 to 20 minutes or till vegetables are tender.
- Flour and water should be mixed inside a small-sized bowl and then added to the stew to thicken it. This should take about 5-10 minutes. It's best practice to get rid of the bay leaf prior to actually serving. Remove from the griddle and serve.

13. Venison Mostaccioli Casserole

(Preparation time: 10 minutes | Cooking time: 1 hour 10 minutes | Servings: 8 | Difficulty: Medium)

Per serving: Calories 417, Total fat 12g, Protein 31g, Carbs 38g

Ingredients:

- 1 pound of ground venison
- 1 (16-ounce) package of mostaccioli or medium-sized tube pasta
- 1 tablespoon of olive oil
- ¼ teaspoon of dried basil
- 1 chopped yellow onion
- 1 (15-ounces) can of tomato sauce
- ⅛ teaspoon of garlic powder
- 3 cups of grated Mozzarella cheese
- Salt & pepper to taste
- ¼ cup of grated Parmesan cheese

Instructions:

- Grease a 9-by-13-inch baking dish with a little oil.
- Bring to a boil a big pot of lightly salted water. Add the pasta & cook for around 8 to 10 minutes, till it is al dente. Drain the pasta and save it.
- Preheat the griddle at medium heat.
- During the meantime, put the olive oil inside a pan on the griddle. Stir in the onion and cook for about 5 minutes, till it is soft and clear. Add the deer meat and cook for about 10 minutes, till it is crumbly and no longer pink. If you need to, drain. Mix in the basil, garlic powder, & tomato sauce. Add salt and pepper to taste, then remove from the griddle.
- Put the casserole together by spreading a layer of the venison sauce on the bottom of the dish that has been set up for baking. Sprinkle Parmesan cheese on the sauce, and then put cooked pasta on top. Layer the sauce, pasta, and 1/2 of the mozzarella on top. Repeat the layers with the rest of the ingredients, completing with a layer of mozzarella cheese. Use aluminum foil to cover the dish. Shift the dish on the griddle.
- Cook for around 20 minutes. Take off the foil cover and cook for about 10 minutes more or till the cheese topping is light gold.

14. Venison Meatloaf

(Preparation time: 15 minutes | Cooking time: 50 minutes | Servings: 4 | Difficulty: Easy)
Per serving: Calories 220, Total fat 5g, Protein 29g, Carbs 15g

Ingredients:

- 2 tablespoons of brown sugar divided
- ½ teaspoon of dried minced onion flakes
- 1-pound ground venison
- 1 dash of cinnamon
- ½ teaspoon of spicy brown mustard
- 8 crumbled saltine crackers
- 1 large beaten egg
- 1 dash of paprika
- ½ teaspoon of garlic powder
- ¼ teaspoon of dried cilantro
- 3 tablespoons of ketchup
- ¼ teaspoon of ground thyme

Instructions:

- Preheat the griddle at medium heat and coat the griddle top using cooking spray.
- Inside a bowl, mix the deer meat, egg, crackers, and 1 tablespoon of brown sugar. Mix together mustard, cinnamon, garlic powder, cilantro, onion flakes, thyme, and paprika, and then season with these ingredients. Pat the combination into a 9x9-inch pan or a loaf pan and move to the griddle.
- Cook for about 40 minutes on the griddle that has already been heated.
- Stir the last tablespoon of brown sugar into the ketchup. Spread the mixture on top of your meatloaf and put it back on the griddle for 10 more minutes.

15. Sweet and Spicy Cocktail Meatballs

(Preparation time: 15 minutes | Cooking time: 30 minutes | Servings: 4 | Difficulty: Easy)

Per serving: Calories 727, Total fat 32g, Protein 25g, Carbs 69g

Ingredients:

- 1 egg
- ⅛ teaspoon of ground black pepper
- 1 pound of ground beef
- 1 (12 ounces) bottle of chile sauce

- ½ cup of dry bread crumbs
- 1 teaspoon of salt
- ¼ cup of milk
- ½ teaspoon of Worcestershire sauce
- 1 tablespoon of snipped fresh parsley
- ¼ cup of shortening
- 1 ¼ cups of grape jelly
- ⅓ cup of minced onion

Instructions:

- Mix the dry bread crumbs, ground beef, and milk inside a large-sized bowl. Mix in the onion, pepper, Worcestershire sauce, parsley, salt, egg, and onion powder. Mix everything well.
- Preheat the griddle at medium heat.
- Make 1-inch meatballs out of the beef mixture. Melt the shortening on the in a large pan and brown the meatballs.
- Mix the grape jelly and chile sauce inside a medium-sized saucepan, stirring every so often, till the jelly is melted.
- Pour the sauce over the meatballs as they are browning, and let them cook for around 30 minutes or till they are fully cooked.

16. Sloppy Does

(Preparation time: 10 minutes | Cooking time: 25 minutes | Servings: 4 | Difficulty: Easy)

Per serving: Calories 175, Total fat 4g, Protein 24g, Carbs 11g

Ingredients:

- 1 clove of diced garlic
- 1 teaspoon of olive oil
- 1 seeded and diced jalapeno pepper
- 2 teaspoons of molasses
- 1 pound of ground venison
- 1 teaspoon of prepared yellow mustard
- ½ cup of ketchup

Instructions:

- Preheat the griddle at medium heat.
- On the griddle, heat the olive oil inside a skillet. Brown the ground venison and jalapeno pepper inside the hot oil, stirring frequently, for about 10 minutes or till the meat is crumbly and thus no longer pink. Mix the venison with the ketchup, molasses, garlic, and yellow mustard. Bring the mixture to boil, then turn the griddle heat down to low. Let it cook for at least ten minutes.

17. Bison Stew

(Preparation time: 10 minutes | Cooking time: 1 hour 25 minutes | Servings: 6 | Difficulty: Easy)

Per serving: Calories 277, Total fat 10g, Protein 36g, Carbs 8g

Ingredients:

- ½ cup of minced celery
- 2 tablespoons of canola oil
- ½ teaspoon of ground black pepper
- 1 tablespoon of canola oil
- 2 pounds of bison meat, cut into one-inch cubes
- 1 (8 ounces) can of tomato sauce
- 1 cup of minced yellow onion
- 2 tablespoons of flour
- 1 cup of water
- 2 cloves of minced garlic
- 2 tablespoons of white wine
- 4 cups of low-sodium chicken broth
- 3 whole cloves
- 2 tablespoons of chopped fresh parsley
- 1 teaspoon of salt
- ¼ teaspoon of ground thyme

Instructions:

- Preheat the griddle at medium heat.

- On the griddle, heat 2 tablespoons of canola oil inside a Dutch oven. Brown the bison in the oil for around 2 to 3 minutes on each side and then set aside. Pour 1 tablespoon of canola oil into the Dutch oven. Cook the onion & celery in the oil, stirring often, till they are soft, which should take about 5 minutes. Cook and stir for another around 2 to 3 minutes with the garlic. Scatter the flour on the mixture and mix to cover. Mix in the broth, parsley, water, tomato sauce, pepper, wine, salt, cloves, and thyme, and bring to boil. Add the bison back into the mix and stir it all together. Turn down the heat of griddle to low, cover, and let the meat simmer for about an hour or till it is soft enough to cut with a fork.

18. Bison Burgers

(Preparation time: 10 minutes | Cooking time: 20 minutes | Servings: 4 | Difficulty: Easy)

Per serving: Calories 393, Total fat 14g, Protein 33g, Carbs 34g

Ingredients:

- 4 slices of American cheese
- 1 pound of ground bison
- 3 tablespoons of Worcestershire sauce
- 1 pinch of ground black pepper
- 4 dashes of hot sauce
- 1 egg
- 1 pinch of granulated garlic
- ½ cup of panko bread crumbs
- Olive oil cooking spray
- 4 split and toasted hamburger buns

Instructions:

- Preheat the griddle at medium heat and coat the griddle top using cooking spray.

- Mix the bison, egg, garlic, bread crumbs, hot sauce, Worcestershire sauce, and pepper together using your hand inside a large-sized bowl. Shape the mixture into 4 patties. Put the patties on a pan for baking. Cover using aluminum foil and put in the fridge for about 15 minutes till it's cold.

- Spray the patties using cooking spray and cook them on a hot griddle for about 5 minutes on each side or till they are hot and the middle is still a little pink. Add a slice of cheese to the top of each patty and cook for another 2 minutes or till the cheese melts. If you put an instant-read temperature gauge in the middle, it should show 140 degrees F.

- Put patties between two toasted halves of a bun.

19. Elk Shepherd's Pie

(Preparation time: 10 minutes | Cooking time: 1 hour 10 minutes | Servings: 6 | Difficulty: Medium)

Per serving: Calories 358, Total fat 9g, Protein 15g, Carbs 37g

Ingredients:

- 2 cups of frozen mixed veggies
- 1 small chopped onion
- ½ cup of half-and-half cream
- 4 peeled and cubed large potatoes
- ½ pound of ground elk meat
- Salt and pepper to taste
- ¼ teaspoon of Italian seasoning
- 1 peeled and diced parsnip
- ¼ teaspoon of garlic powder
- 2 tablespoons of butter
- 1 tablespoon of melted butter

Instructions:

- Cover the potatoes with salty water inside a large pot. Bring to the boil, then turn the flame down to medium, cover, and simmer for about 20 minutes or till the potatoes are soft. Drain the potatoes and let them steam dry for a minute or two. Mash the potatoes using salt, pepper, two tablespoons of butter, and half-and-half.
- Preheat the griddle at medium heat and coat the griddle top using cooking spray.
- In the meantime, stir the elk meat, salt, Italian seasoning, and pepper together inside a skillet on the griddle for about 5 minutes, until it is crumbly and no longer pink. Spread cooked elk meat in a pie plate or baking dish that's 9 inches in diameter, and put the skillet back on the griddle.
- Put the parsnip, onion, and garlic powder in the skillet. Add salt and pepper to taste, and cook for about 10 minutes or till the turnip is soft. Mix in the mixed vegetables and cook for 5 more minutes. Then, spread them over the elk in the pie plate. The last

step is to spread the mashed potatoes equally over the top and brush them with the melted butter.

- Cook on the hot griddle for about 30 minutes or till the potatoes start to turn golden brown. Serve hot.

20. Honey-Orange Bison Back Ribs

(Preparation time: 10 minutes | Cooking time: 1 hour 20 minutes | Servings: 6 | Difficulty: Medium)

Per serving: Calories 263, Total fat 3g, Protein 35g, Carbs 23g

Ingredients:

- 1 ½ cups of orange juice
- 5 pounds of bison back ribs, cut into two- to three-rib portions
- 2 (12-ounce) bottles of chili sauce
- ⅓ cup of cider vinegar
- 2 teaspoons of finely shredded orange zest
- ¼ cup of honey
- 1 teaspoon of salt
- ½ teaspoon of black pepper
- 4 cloves of minced garlic
- ½ cup of finely chopped onion

Instructions:

- Put bison back ribs inside a pot that holds 4 to 6 quarts. Put water on top. Bring it to boil, then lower the flame. Simmer, covered, for around 1 hour or till tender. Drain and let cool for around 30 minutes. Bison back ribs should be put inside a large plastic bag that can be sealed and set inside a shallow dish.

- Mix chili sauce, salt, orange juice, honey, orange zest, onion, garlic, vinegar, and pepper inside a large-sized bowl to make the marinade. Pour three cups over the bison back ribs. Bison back ribs should be marinated in the fridge for 4 to 24 hours, with the bag turned every so often. Cover the rest of the marinade and chill till you need it. Drain the bison back ribs and save the marinade to brush on the ribs as they cook on the griddle.

- Preheat the griddle at medium heat and coat the griddle top using cooking spray.

- Put the bison back ribs on the griddle rack over the drip pan. Cover and cook for around 15 to 20 minutes, or until the meat is cooked all the way through, brushing once using some of the marinade that has been drained; throw away any marinade that was used to brush the meat.

- Put the marinade you didn't use to marinate or brush the meat inside a medium-sized saucepan. Bring to the boil. Simmer for 10 minutes with the lid off. Serve with bison back ribs.

21. Elk Chili

(Preparation time: 20 minutes | Cooking time: 30 minutes | Servings: 6 | Difficulty: Easy)

Per serving: Calories 307, Total fat 2g, Protein 28g, Carbs 45g

Ingredients:

- 2 (10 ounces) cans of tomato sauce
- 1 ½ teaspoons of ground cumin
- 1 teaspoon of black pepper
- 1 ½ pounds of ground elk meat
- 1 (4 ounces) can of diced green chiles (Optional)
- 2 large diced yellow onions
- 1 teaspoon of salt
- 1 (14.5 ounces) can of Italian-style stewed tomatoes
- ½ cup of brown sugar
- 1 (15 ounces) can of kidney beans, drained
- 1 ½ tablespoons of chili powder
- 1 teaspoon of dried oregano

Instructions:

- Preheat the griddle at medium heat.
- Cook the ground elk and onion inside a large-sized deep skillet on the griddle till evenly browned. Remove any excess grease.
- Stir together the tomato sauce, kidney beans, stewed tomatoes, and green chilies in the skillet with the meat. Chili powder, oregano, cumin, pepper, salt, and brown sugar to taste. Simmer for at least one hour, covered, on the griddle.

22. Roast Pheasant

(Preparation time: 20 minutes | Cooking time: 2 hours 10 minutes | Servings: 4 | Difficulty: Easy)

Per serving: Calories 640, Total fat 43g, Protein 45g, Carbs 5g

Ingredients:

- 2 sprigs of rosemary, leaves chopped and stripped
- 1 whole cleaned pheasant
- 1 cup of olive oil
- Salt & ground black pepper to taste
- 1 tablespoon of chopped fresh thyme

Instructions:

- Preheat the griddle at medium heat.
- Set aside thyme and rosemary in a liquid measure with olive oil.
- Season the inside and outside of the pheasant using salt and black pepper. Place inside a roasting pan with a tight fit. Spread herb oil over the pheasant.
- Cook for around 1 hour in a preheated griddle, then cover using aluminum foil and continue cooking till an instant-read thermometer placed into the widest part of the thigh, close to the bone, recognizes 180 degrees F, around 1 hour more. Every 30 minutes, baste the pheasant using pan juices.
- Remove from the griddle, cover using a doubled sheet of the aluminum foil, and set aside for around 10 minutes before slicing.

23. Slow Roasted Rabbit

(Preparation time: 20 minutes | Cooking time: 1 hour 40 minutes | Servings: 4 | Difficulty: Easy)

Per serving: Calories 626, Total fat 31g, Protein 64g, Carbs 22g

Ingredients:

- ¼ cup of vegetable oil
- 1 (3 pounds) of rabbit, washed and sliced into pieces
- 1 tablespoon of paprika
- ¾ cup of ketchup
- 4 teaspoons of white sugar
- 1 tablespoon of ground black pepper
- 1 ¾ teaspoons of salt
- 1 chopped onion

- 1 ½ tablespoons of Worcestershire sauce
- 1 cup of water
- 1 chopped clove of garlic

Instructions:

- Preheat the griddle at medium heat.
- Season the rabbit using pepper and salt.
- Inside a large-sized skillet on the griddle, heat the vegetable oil. Cook the rabbit in hot oil till it is brown from all sides. Put the mixture inside a 9x13-inch baking pan.
- Inside a medium-sized mixing bowl, combine paprika, onion, water, sugar, ketchup, Worcestershire sauce, and garlic; mix well, then sprinkle over rabbit.
- Cook uncovered on the griddle with a baking pan for around 90 minutes, basting oftenly, till very tender. An instant-read temperature gauge inserted near the bone should register at least 160 degrees F.

24. Chipotle Bison Chili

(Preparation time: 10 minutes | Cooking time: 40 minutes | Servings: 8 | Difficulty: Easy)
Per serving: Calories 343, Total fat 15g, Protein 26g, Carbs 30g
Ingredients:

- 1 pound of ground beef
- ¼ cup of warm water
- 2 tablespoons of olive oil, divided
- 2 minced cloves of garlic
- 1 (8 ounces) can of tomato sauce
- 3 tablespoons of chili powder
- 1 pound of ground bison
- 1 (15 ounces) can of kidney beans, drained
- 1 chopped green bell pepper
- 2 tablespoons of corn flour
- ½ chopped large onion

- 1 (28 ounces) can of crushed tomatoes
- 1 teaspoon of white sugar
- 2 tablespoons of chipotle chile powder
- 1 tablespoon of ground cumin
- 1 teaspoon of salt, or more to taste
- 1 (10 ounces) can of diced tomatoes with the green chile peppers
- 2 tablespoons of Worcestershire sauce
- 1 (8 ounces) can of whole kernel corn, drained

Instructions:

- Preheat the griddle at medium heat.
- Inside a large-sized saucepan on the griddle, heat the oil. Around 5 to 7 minutes, cook and mix beef and bison till browned and crumbly. Grease should be drained and discarded. Shift meat inside a bowl.
- Within the same saucepan, heat up the remaining olive oil on the griddle. Cook till the onion, green bell pepper, and garlic are translucent, about 3 minutes. Incorporate the cooked meat. Stir in the chipotle powder, chili powder, and cumin. Stir once more. Add the crushed tomatoes, Worcestershire sauce, corn, tomato sauce, kidney beans, diced tomatoes, 1 teaspoon of salt, & sugar. Continue to stir the chili for at least around 25 minutes.
- Inside a mixing bowl, combine warm water & corn flour. Pour the mixture into the chili. Continue to cook till the sauce has thickened, around 10 minutes more. Season using salt and pepper.

25. Buffalo Veggie Quinoa Meatloaf

(Preparation time: 10 minutes | Cooking time: 1 hour 20 minutes | Servings: 4 | Difficulty: Easy)

Per serving: Calories 265, Total fat 8g, Protein 25g, Carbs 22g

Ingredients:

- 1 small chopped sweet yellow onion
- ½ cup of water
- 1 tablespoon of minced garlic
- 1 pinch of dried basil
- ¼ cup of quinoa

- 1 cup of chopped kale
- 1 tablespoon of olive oil
- 1 teaspoon of ground black pepper
- 2 eggs
- 1 chopped sweet potato
- 1 pinch of dried thyme
- ½ chopped red bell pepper
- 1 tablespoon of Worcestershire sauce
- 1 tablespoon of ketchup
- 1 pound of ground buffalo meat
- 1 ½ teaspoons of salt
- 1 pinch of dried oregano
- 1 tablespoon of barbeque sauce

Instructions:

- Preheat the griddle at medium heat. Coat a 9x5-inch loaf pan using cooking spray.
- Inside a saucepan, bring water and quinoa to the boil. Reduce the flame to medium, cover, & simmer for 10 to 15 minutes or till the quinoa is tender and the water has been absorbed.
- Inside a skillet on the griddle, heat the olive oil; cook and stir the onion, kale, sweet potato, and red bell pepper till tender, around 10 to 15 minutes.
- Inside a mixing bowl, combine basil, buffalo meat, salt, eggs, oregano, Worcestershire sauce, black pepper, garlic, ketchup, and thyme. Mix in the vegetable and quinoa mixtures with the buffalo mixture. Place the mixture in the greased loaf pan and cover using a thin layer of bbq sauce.
- Cook for around 1 hour in the griddle till the center is no longer pink. In the center, an instant-read thermometer must read at least 160 degrees F.

26. Garlic Rabbit

(Preparation time: 10 minutes | Cooking time: 25 minutes | Servings: 4 | Difficulty: Easy)

Per serving: Calories 540, Total fat 25g, Protein 52g, Carbs 12g

Ingredients:

- 1 cup of salt-free garlic marinade
- 1 (3 pounds) of rabbit, cleaned & cut into pieces

Instructions:

- After washing and drying the rabbit parts, place them inside a large resealable plastic bag. After adding the marinade, seal out the bag. Allow 2 to 8 hours or for overnight in the refrigerator to marinate the rabbit, turning the bag over several times to coat it with the marinade.
- Preheat the griddle at medium flame and coat the griddle top using cooking spray.
- Remove the rabbit from marinade and shake off any excess liquid; discard the marinade.

- Place the rabbit chunks on the griddle. Cook for around 12 to 15 minutes per side or till the rabbit has good grill marks, the flesh underneath is no longer pink, and the juices run clear. The internal temperature of the thickest part of the meat must reach at least 160 degrees F on an instant-read thermometer.

27. Rabbit Loin Cigars

(Preparation time: 10 minutes | Cooking time: 30 minutes | Servings: 2 | Difficulty: Medium)

Per serving: Calories 645, Total fat 57g, Protein 45g, Carbs 38g

Ingredients:

- 1 teaspoon of minced shallot
- 1 cup of morel mushrooms
- ¼ sheet of frozen puff pastry, thawed
- 6 ounces of rabbit loin
- 1 egg yolk, beaten
- 2 teaspoons of vegetable oil
- Salt and pepper to taste
- ½ cup of beef or veal demi-glace
- 1 tablespoon of butter
- 3 spears of white asparagus, trimmed

Instructions:

- Preheat the griddle at medium heat. Line a baking sheet with parchment paper.
- Heat the oil inside a small skillet over medium-high heat. the salt, mushrooms, shallot, and pepper. Cook, stirring frequently, for around 5 to 10 minutes or till the mushrooms have broken down into a paste. Remove the pan from the heat and leave it to cool slightly.
- On a clean work surface, roll out the puff pastry to fit the length of the rabbit loin. Apply the mushroom paste to the entire surface. In the center of the plate, arrange the asparagus alongside the rabbit loin.
- Seal the pastry cylinder around the rabbit and asparagus by pinching the ends. Place the pastry on the prepared baking sheet and cover it with egg yolk.
- Cook on the griddle with the lid for around 10 to 15 minutes or till the pastry is a rich golden color. Allow for 5 minutes of cooling after removing from the griddle. The meat's internal temperature should be at least 145 degrees F.

- While the rabbit is cooking, warm the demi-glace inside a small-sized skillet on the griddle. Remove the butter from the griddle once it has melted and become hot.
- To serve, cut the puff pastry in half crosswise and place it in the center of a serving plate. Distribute the sauce on the platter.

28. Rabbit with Sage and Lemon

(Preparation time: 10 minutes | Cooking time: 40 minutes | Servings: 6 | Difficulty: Medium)

Per serving: Calories 303, Total fat 13g, Protein 32g, Carbs 11g

Ingredients:

- 3 zucchinis
- 750g rabbit fillets

For the marinade:

- 2 garlic cloves
- Freshly ground pepper
- 1 lemon
- 100 ml of olive oil
- 4 sprigs of fresh sage
- 80 ml lemon
- Salt

Instructions:

- Let us start with the marinade.
- The lemon should be peeled and washed. Blanch your lemon peel in boiling water for about 2 minutes before rinsing in cool water.
- Finely chop the garlic, lemon peel, and leaves from two sage sprigs.
- After adding the olive oil, season with pepper and salt to taste.
- Slice the zucchini into slices with a vegetable slicer.
- Place the rabbit pieces in one bowl and the zucchini slices in another.
- Distribute the marinade among the bowls and leave to marinate for 2 hours.
- Preheat the griddle at medium heat and coat the griddle top using cooking spray.
- Skewer the rabbit flesh with brochette sticks.

- To avoid charring or burning, soak wooden skewers in water for an hour before using them.
- Cook the rabbit meat for about 5 to 8 minutes on each side on the griddle.
- Cook the zucchini slices on the griddle for 4 to 5 minutes as well.

29. Greek Rabbit

(Preparation time: 10 minutes | Cooking time: 45 minutes | Servings: 4 | Difficulty: Easy)

Per serving: Calories 567, Total fat 30g, Protein 62g, Carbs 2g

Ingredients:

- ¼ cup of olive oil
- 1 (3 pounds) of rabbit, cut into pieces
- 4 whole allspice berries
- 2 bay leaves
- Warm water to cover
- 1 lemon, juiced
- ½ teaspoon of oregano
- 1 teaspoon of salt
- ½ cup of white wine

Instructions:

- Preheat the griddle at medium heat.
- Heat 1/4 cup of olive oil inside a large-sized saucepan on the griddle over medium heat. In hot oil, brown the rabbit pieces evenly. Add the bay leaves, salt, oregano, allspice berries, and lemon juice to the pot. Pour the white wine over the rabbit. Cook for 4 to 5 minutes after bringing the mixture to a simmer. Fill the pot with enough water to submerge the rabbit completely.
- Cook for about 40 minutes, stirring occasionally, till the rabbit is warmed through and the liquid has evaporated.

30. Caribbean Rabbit

(Preparation time: 15 minutes | Cooking time: 3 hours 10 minutes | Servings: 6 | Difficulty: Easy)

Per serving: Calories 621, Total fat 35g, Protein 13g, Carbs 56g

Ingredients:

- 1 rabbit, cut into small pieces
- Caribbean spices
- 2 to 3 garlic cloves
- Fresh mushrooms
- Salt
- 1 lime and 1 lemon
- Olive oil

Instructions:

- Inside a mixing bowl, combine two spoons of olive oil, lime and lemon juice, minced garlic, salt, and Caribbean spices to make the marinade for the rabbit (mix of black pepper, caraway, cayenne pepper, chili, paprika, coriander, green pepper, turmeric, savory, minced laurel leaves, grated lime peel).
- After washing the rabbit parts, add them to the marinade. Refrigerate the meat for several hours, stirring every now and then.
- Preheat the griddle at medium heat once you're ready to cook the rabbit chunks.
- Spray the griddle top using cooking spray.
- Cook on the griddle till the meat is thoroughly cooked. After 5 minutes, flip the meat.
- Allow for 5 minutes before turning and cooking for another 3 minutes on the first side, or till the meat is well cooked on both sides.
- Wash the mushrooms in the beef marinade till the sauce is completely reduced.
- Serve your grilled Caribbean rabbit on a bed of mushrooms.
- Enjoy!

4-Week Meal Plan

Week 1

Days	Breakfast	Lunch	Snacks	Dinner
1	Gorgonzola and Figs Toast	Roasted Sheet Pan Salmon with Spring Vegetables and Pesto	Parmesan-Herb Popcorn	Seared Spicy Citrus Chicken
2	Breakfast Enchiladas	Wine and Thyme Turkey Stew	Apple Cobbler	Tuna Meatloaf with Lemon and Capers
3	Veggie Breakfast Cakes	Italian Hamburgers	Southwestern-Style Stuffed Peppers	Roasted Lamb with Root Vegetables
4	Breakfast Sandwich with Bacon and Swiss Cheese	Roast Beef Stuffed with Spinach and Speck	Irish Coffee Pie	Texas-Style Brisket
5	Italian Egg, Sausage and Cheese Crunch Wrap	Turkey Breast Noodles with Ginger and Parsley	Smashed Cheddar Bacon Baby Potatoes	Spinach Salad with Tomato Melts
6	Fluffy Blueberry Pancakes	Pork Skewers with Avocado and Cherry Tomatoes	Soft Gingerbread Cookies	Asian Turkey Burgers
7	Hearty Breakfast Muffins	Scallops with Lemony Salsa Verde	Caramel Pecan Brownie	Beef Chili

Week 2

Days	Breakfast	Lunch	Snacks	Dinner
1	Breakfast English Muffin Strata	Tofu Skewers with Spicy Peanut Sauce	Sausage Mini Rolls	Turkey Breast in Citrus Fruits and Rhubarb Sauce
2	Charred Bread with Ricotta and Cherry Salsa	Spiced Snapper with Mango and Red Onion Salad	Caramel Bananas	Ratatouille
3	Mini Breakfast Quiches	Goulash	Loaded Potatoes	Swordfish with Corn Salsa
4	Whole meal and Cocoa Pancake	Pears and Pine Nuts Stuffed Chicken	Chocolate Chip Mint Cookies	Moroccan-Spiced Rack of Lamb
5	Veggie Breakfast Cakes	Middle Eastern Turkey Kibbeh Burgers	Crispy Kale Chips	Grilled Ranch Pork Chops with Peach Jalapeno Salsa
6	Oatmeal Breakfast Bars	Sweet Mesquite Seasoned Chicken Breasts	Atomic Buffalo Turds	Spicy Tofu and Pork Burgers
7	Breakfast Burritos with Green Salsa	Lamb with Mint Orange Sauce	Brownie Bread Pudding	Cedar-Plank Salmon with Mango Salsa

Week 3

Days	Breakfast	Lunch	Snacks	Dinner
1	Fluffy Blueberry Pancakes	Teriyaki Chicken and Veggie Rice Bowls	Lemon Bars	Chicken Marsala Burgers
2	Breakfast Sandwich with Bacon and Swiss Cheese	Rack of Beef with Potatoes and Mushrooms	Loaded Nachos	Chicken Satay in Almond Butter Sauce
3	Ricotta Cheese and Pistachio Sandwich	Bulgarian Burgers	Stuffing Turkey Bacon Balls	Cumin Spiced Turkey Breast
4	Avocado and Egg Breakfast Burrito	Roasted Stuffed Rainbow Trout with Brown Butter	Caramelized Bourbon Pears	Glazed Tofu Steaks with Mango Salsa
5	Breakfast Potato Boats	Soy Cheese and Bell Pepper Gazpacho	Southwest Chicken Drumsticks	Crunchy Chicken Burgers
6	Sausage and Veggie Scramble	Bean & Chile Burgers	Cherry Cobbler	Parsley Herbed Fish Stew
7	Breakfast Enchiladas	Maple Bourbon Turkey	Bacon Cheddar Slider	Buttermilk Chicken

Week 4

Days	Breakfast	Lunch	Snacks	Dinner
1	Italian Egg, Sausage and Cheese Crunch Wrap	Classical Chicken Meatballs in Hot Sauce	Apple Pear Crisp	Romaine Salad with Bacon & Blue Cheese
2	Breakfast Burritos with Green Salsa	Moroccan Spiced Pork Tenderloin with Creamy Harissa Sauce	Blueberry Buckle Coffee Cake	Citrusy Clams with Tomatoes & Chickpeas
3	Charred Bread with Ricotta and Cherry Salsa	Roasted Halibut with Tartar Sauce	Tortilla Pizza	Classic Beef Stew
4	Gorgonzola and Figs Toast	Tuscan-Style Steak with Crispy Potatoes	Chewy Peanut Butter Cookies	Grilled Chicken with Fruit Salsa
5	Ricotta Cheese and Pistachio Sandwich	Tex-Mex Burgers	Chili Con Queso	Halibut Fillets with Spinach and Olives
6	Oatmeal Breakfast Bars	Lamb Loaf	Loaded Tater Tots	Sliced Beef with Asparagus and Honey Sauce
7	Breakfast English Muffin Strata	Gorgonzola and Potatoes Gratin	Pumpkin Pie	Double-Cut Grilled Pork Chop with Sweet & Sour Peaches

Conclusion

You make it all the way to the end, which is fantastic. If you like to start your day with a hearty breakfast, you should consider purchasing an outdoor gas griddle. These plates are great because they allow you to cook at low temperatures without worrying about flare-ups or burns. They also have safety features that automatically shut off when they detect overheating, removing the risk of unintentional fires when cooking for a large group.

The Griddle is an excellent tool that will make your life easier and less stressful. Whether you're cooking for family or friends, the gas griddle can come in handy. On one griddle, you can cook everything from eggs and pancakes to grilled sandwiches and burgers!

Your Griddle can be used for a variety of purposes for many years to come thanks to the high-quality industrial materials it is constructed from. The powder-coated steel used to make the griddle's frame ensures that it will last for years. The stainless steel construction of the burners guarantees years of reliable service and safe cooking conditions.

The Gas Griddle is ideal for families who enjoy perfectly prepared backyard classics like burgers, steaks, and vegetables, as well as substantial breakfasts, because it is large enough to cook all of the components of a whole meal simultaneously. Make everyone's eggs, bacon, hash browns, and pancakes at the same time.

Hope this book has answered all your queries regarding the outdoor gas griddle. Good luck!

Recipes Index

Apple Cobbler; 88

Apple Pear Crisp; 98

Apple, Rocket, and Pistachio Grilled Chicken; 163

Asian Salmon Burgers; 56

Asian Turkey Burgers; 45

Asparagus Wrapped in Bacon; 108

Atomic Buffalo Turds; 112

Avocado and Egg Breakfast Burrito; 29

Bacon Cheddar Slider; 92

Bacon-Gouda Burgers; 57

Balsamic-Glazed Veggie Kabobs; 77

Barbecue Cheese Burgers; 44

BBQ Chili Smoked Turkey Breast; 153

Bean & Chile Burgers; 58

Beef Chili; 185

Beef Meatballs in Sweet and Sour Sauce; 194

Beef Steak with Curry Sauce and Pine Nuts; 168

Bison Burgers; 212

Bison Stew; 211

Blue Stuffed Buffalo Burger; 204

Blueberry Buckle Coffee Cake; 111

Breaded Pheasant Nuggets; 198

Breakfast Burritos with Green Salsa; 34

Breakfast Enchiladas; 41

Breakfast English Muffin Strata; 35

Breakfast Potato Boats; 40

Breakfast Sandwich with Bacon and Swiss Cheese; 25

Brownie Bread Pudding; 94

Buffalo Meatloaf; 201

Buffalo Veggie Quinoa Meatloaf; 219

Bulgarian Burgers; 54

Caramel Bananas; 89

Caramel Pecan Brownie; 101

Caramelized Bourbon Pears; 105

Caribbean Rabbit; 224

Cauliflower and Spicy Cheddar Soufflé; 83

Cedar-Plank Salmon with Mango Salsa; 122

Charred Bread with Ricotta and Cherry Salsa; 33

Cherry Cobbler; 102

Chewy Peanut Butter Cookies; 92

Chicken Marsala Burgers; 58

Chicken Satay in Almond Butter Sauce; 151

Chili Con Queso; 100

Chipotle Bison Chili; 218

Chocolate Chip Mint Cookies; 96

Citrusy Clams with Tomatoes & Chickpeas; 132

Citrusy Goose Breast; 149

Classic Beef Stew; 175

Classical Chicken Meatballs in Hot Sauce; 143

Colorado Buffalo Chili; 202

Corn Cakes; 87

Crab Cakes; 135

Creamy Grilled Potato Salad; 60

Creole Chicken Stuffed with Cheese & Peppers; 142

Crispy Kale Chips; 91

Crunchy Chicken Burgers; 51

Cuban Frita Burgers; 46

Cumin Chili Potato Wedges; 85

Cumin Spiced Turkey Breast; 159

Deer Jerky; 203

Deer Poppers; 199

Double-Cut Grilled Pork Chop with Sweet & Sour Peaches; 179

Drunk Deer Chili; 200

Duck Adobo; 165

Duck with Soy, Honey, and Ginger; 157

Easy Fried Rice; 61

Egg White Breakfast Bites; 31

Eggplant and Ricotta Bundles; 68

Elk Chili; 215

Elk Shepherd's Pie; 213

Fluffy Blueberry Pancakes; 37

French Toast Sticks; 26

Garlic Rabbit; 221

Garlic, Bacon & Lemon Cauliflower Steaks; 82

Garlicky Salmon with Avocado Salsa; 134

German Burgers; 47

Glazed Tofu Steaks with Mango Salsa; 76

Goose and Kraut; 152

Gorgonzola and Figs Toast; 41

Gorgonzola and Potatoes Gratin; 78

Goulash; 195

Greek Rabbit; 224

Green Beans in Mustard Sauce; 62

Gremolata Swordfish Skewers; 137

Grilled Chicken with Fruit Salsa; 144

Grilled Potato Chips with Lemon Mustard Sauce; 73

Grilled Ranch Pork Chops with Peach Jalapeno Salsa; 170

Grilled Southwestern Lamb; 192

Grilled Summer Burgers; 53

Habanero-Marinated Pork Chops; 189

Halibut Fillets with Lemon and Butter Sauce; 140

Halibut Fillets with Spinach and Olives; 138

Hearty Breakfast Muffins; 42

Honey-Orange Bison Back Ribs; 214

Irish Coffee Pie; 106

Italian Egg, Sausage and Cheese Crunch Wrap; 38

Italian Hamburgers; 45

Key West Burgers; 50

Lamb Chops in Soy Sauce; 190

Lamb Loaf; 182

Lamb Lollipops with Mango Chutney; 172

Lamb Lollipops with Yuzu Aioli; 191

Lamb with Mint Orange Sauce; 181

Lemon Bars; 109

Lemon Ginger Chicken with Fruit Salsa; 164

Loaded Nachos; 97

Loaded Potatoes; 114

Loaded Tater Tots; 93

Lobster Tails with Citrus Butter; 118

Maple Bourbon Turkey; 154
Marinated Smoked Turkey Breast; 165
Mexican Burgers; 52
Mexican Shrimp; 131
Middle Eastern Turkey Kibbeh Burgers; 48
Mini Breakfast Quiches; 35
Moroccan Chicken; 150
Moroccan Spiced Pork Tenderloin with Creamy Harissa Sauce; 171
Moroccan-Spiced Rack of Lamb; 183
Oatmeal Breakfast Bars; 30
Open-Faced Lone Star Burgers; 50
Oysters with Spiced Tequila Butter; 135
Oysters with Tequila Butter Skillet; 127
Parmesan-Garlic Asparagus; 86
Parmesan-Herb Popcorn; 109
Parsley Herbed Fish Stew; 128
Pears and Pine Nuts Stuffed Chicken; 156
Peas and Cheddar Pie; 67
Pheasant Poppers; 198
Porcini Mushrooms, Garlic and Bacon Omelet; 27
Pork Chops Stuffed with Cheese; 188
Pork Skewers with Apple and Feta; 187
Pork Skewers with Avocado and Cherry Tomatoes; 180
Pumpkin Pie; 91
Rabbit Loin Cigars; 222
Rabbit with Sage and Lemon; 223
Rack of Beef with Potatoes and Mushrooms; 176
Ratatouille; 75

Ricotta Cheese and Pistachio Sandwich; 30
Roast Beef Stuffed with Spinach and Speck; 169
Roast Pheasant; 215
Roasted Broccoli with Parmesan; 64
Roasted Duck; 161
Roasted Halibut with Tartar Sauce; 126
Roasted Lamb with Root Vegetables; 174
Roasted Sheet Pan Salmon with Spring Vegetables and Pesto; 116
Roasted Stuffed Rainbow Trout with Brown Butter; 125
Romaine Salad with Bacon & Blue Cheese; 69
Sausage and Veggie Scramble; 28
Sausage Mini Rolls; 103
Scallops with Lemony Salsa Verde; 119
Seafood Ceviche; 123
Seekh Kebab Burgers; 55
Sliced Beef with Asparagus and Honey Sauce; 193
Sloppy Does; 210
Slow Roasted Rabbit; 217
Smashed Cheddar Bacon Baby Potatoes; 90
Smoked Cheesy Eggplant; 79
Smoked Trout Burgers with Horseradish and Ricotta; 53
Smothered Pheasant; 197
Soft Gingerbread Cookies; 99
Southwest Chicken Drumsticks; 87
Southwestern-Style Stuffed Peppers; 104
Soy Cheese and Bell Pepper Gazpacho; 72
Spiced Snapper with Mango and Red Onion Salad; 121

Spicy Asian BBQ Shrimp; 117

Spicy Tofu and Pork Burgers; 49

Spinach Salad with Tomato Melts; 62

Stuffed Gouda Chicken Meatloaf; 155

Stuffed Yellow Bell Peppers; 81

Stuffing Turkey Bacon Balls; 100

Sweet and Spicy Cocktail Meatballs; 209

Sweet Mesquite Seasoned Chicken Breasts; 162

Sweet Mustard Calamari; 129

Swordfish with Corn Salsa; 130

Tender & Sweet Chicken Skewers; 148

Tender Pheasants; 204

Teriyaki Chicken and Veggie Rice Bowls; 147

Teriyaki Salmon; 131

Texas-Style Brisket; 178

Tex-Mex Burgers; 54

Thyme Potato Focaccia; 70

Tofu and Ginger Stuffed Yellow Bell Peppers; 71

Tofu Skewers with Spicy Peanut Sauce; 65

Tortilla Pizza; 96

Tuna Meatloaf with Lemon and Capers; 120

Tuna with Pistachio Sauce; 139

Turkey Breast Noodles with Ginger and Parsley; 158

Turkey in Herb Sauce; 146

Tuscan-Style Steak with Crispy Potatoes; 186

Veggie Breakfast Cakes; 39

Venison Fajitas; 205

Venison Meatloaf; 208

Venison Mostaccioli Casserole; 207

Venison Stew; 206

White Wine Shrimp Scampi; 133

Whole meal and Cocoa Pancake; 32

Wild Duck Breast; 145

Wine and Thyme Turkey Stew; 167

Zucchini Almond and Gouda Meatballs; 66

Zucchini and Tomato Quiche; 80

Made in United States
Troutdale, OR
08/13/2023